MONGANGA
PAUL

The Congo Ministry and Martyrdom
of Paul Carlson, M.D.

LOIS CARLSON BRIDGES

Covenant Publications
CHICAGO, ILLINOIS

All quotations from the New Testament are from the New English Bible translation. Quotations from the Old Testament are, generally, from the King James Version.

Covenant Publications
5101 North Francisco Avenue
Chicago, Illinois 60625
(773) 784-3000
www.covchurch.org

First published by Harper & Row.

14 13 12 11 10 09 08 07 06 05 04   6 5 4 3 2 1

ISBN 0-910452-93-8

To Wayne and Lynette

EDITOR'S NOTE

It has been forty years since the death of Dr. Paul Carlson, medical missionary of the Evangelical Covenant Church, who was killed in November 1964 while held prisoner by rebels in Congo.

Monganga Paul was written in 1965 by Lois Carlson Bridges, Dr. Carlson's widow. It is being rereleased as part of a year-long focus on Paul Carlson that not only honors the life and work, but calls each of us to renewed lives of discipleship as followers of Jesus Christ.

A foreword has been written by Glenn R. Palmberg, president of the Evangelical Covenant Church, and an afterword has been added that focuses attention on one of the important legacies of Paul Carlson's work—the Paul Carlson Partnership and its work of rehabilitation and development in Africa and beyond. The preface and acknowledgments by the author are presented as originally published. Changes include additional photographs and textual alterations to update the language.

A special note of thanks goes to Dr. Carlson's home church, Rolling Hills Covenant Church in California, for financial assistance that made reprinting this work possible.

CONTENTS

Foreword ix

Preface xiii

Acknowledgments. xv

CHAPTER I

A Call to Tandala 1

CHAPTER II

A Pattern Forming. 17

CHAPTER III

Operation Doctor 37

CHAPTER IV

So Send I You. 46

CHAPTER V

Arrival in Africa. 54

CHAPTER VI

The Forgotten Corner 68

CHAPTER VII

"No One Ever Comes to Wasolo" 86

CHAPTER VIII

Threatening Days—and a Wedding 100

CHAPTER IX

The River between Us 115

CHAPTER X

November 141

CHAPTER XI

Return to the Ubangi 154

Epilogue 162
Afterword 168
Glossary 173
Maps 178

FOREWORD

It was November 2003. It was my first visit to Africa, and we were touring a hospital in the northwest part of the Democratic Republic of Congo. As we came to the intensive care ward, Bob Thornbloom firmly pushed me across it and into the room beyond. "Glenn," he said, "I don't want you in there. The smell and the germs could make you sick." The Congolese doctor giving the tour apologized: "We wash it, but we have no soap and no disinfectant. We can't get the smell out." No soap and no disinfectant—in a hospital.

I cannot forget that smell. I cannot forget the patients lying on grass mats on metal bed frames, with only the light coming in through the windows—there was no electricity, either. I cannot forget the hospital pharmacy, with a few bottles of tablets set out on a table. I cannot forget the children—the sick ones lying still and weak, their parents keeping watch beside them, and the healthy ones outside laughing and running to escort us on our way. I cannot forget—and I don't want to.

That hospital was established to honor Dr. Paul Carlson after his death in 1964. I saw the image of God in the people there—in the faces of the patients and the doctors, the sick children and the healthy ones. And I could understand in my heart and soul how Paul Carlson loved them so much.

As this is written, the people of northwest Congo are beginning to rebuild their lives following the destruction of six years of civil war. The four hospitals and seventy-three clinics of the Covenant Church of Congo are continuing to care for people in buildings that were stripped and damaged. One of the hospitals has received international recognition for its role in coordinating humanitarian efforts, especially in the fight against HIV/AIDS. This quality and continuity of care even in the very worst of circumstances, and the trained local medical staff who provide it, are legacies of Paul Carlson and the other missionaries who labored there.

There is also a church in northwest Congo—a strong, vibrant, growing church—and it is also a legacy of Paul Carlson and other faithful missionaries. The Communauté Évangélique de l'Ubangi-Mongala (CEUM) now has 178,000 members. It operates the hospitals and clinics, along with elementary and secondary schools, adult Bible schools, and camps. The faith of the people persevered and grew stronger even as their homes, churches, and schools were looted and burned. Together they have become tough in spirit, renewed in strength, and ever more dependent on and committed to Christ.

Paul Carlson did not have a long time in Congo. He served for less than two years all together. Yet the impact of his life and his death upon the Congolese people whom he loved so much was incalculable. He was a true disciple of Jesus Christ—not only believing in him, but following him. Forty years later, people are still being healed—both physically and spiritually—because of him. Even in his home church in North America, the Evangelical Covenant Church, he made a significant impact in the lives and future commitments of many people.

This book is, first of all, a compelling story about a man so real that those who knew him loved him, and the rest of us wish we had known him. It is also a call to examine how God is working in our own lives. It is a call to be not just believers, but followers of Jesus. Paul Carlson never imagined how far his legacy would extend. He simply went where God wanted him to be and did what God wanted him to do, day by day. That is exactly what God asks of each of us.

In reprinting this story for a new generation of disciples, we have added an afterword, which further explores Paul's legacy as it continues and grows today. Here we lay out some ways interested individuals can share directly in the work he left to us, through the Paul Carlson Partnership and its work of rehabilitation and development in Africa and beyond.

Thank God for Paul Carlson, for Lois and their family, and for each and every one of the other missionaries who have given, and continue to give, their full lives for the sake of Christ's love for the Congolese people. May Paul's story, recorded here in this book, enlarge his legacy through each person who reads it and senses in a new way God's unique call upon his or her own life.

GLENN R. PALMBERG

President

The Evangelical Covenant Church

PREFACE

I remember President Kennedy's death—how the details came to us in Africa, how we didn't really know what had happened until a copy of *Time* magazine reached us. Jody LeVahn, the mission nurse, and I were driving back to Wasolo after getting the mail at Yakoma. As Jody drove, I read the magazine account aloud, and I cried as I learned the details for the first time. I recall putting myself in Mrs. Kennedy's shoes and thinking how hard it must be for her.

Now, as I look back at my husband's death—it came just a year and two days after President Kennedy's—I have a difficult time realizing that it has been my story. All the publicity, the pictures, the questions, and the letters of condolence and expressions of good will hardly seem real. Has all this happened to *me*, to *our family?* Of course it has, and when I come back to this realization the way seems hardest.

I tell myself what the widows of the five missionaries killed by the Auca Indians in South America told themselves: "Self-pity is the rot of the soul." I tell myself that the ministry of service that Paul Carlson believed in and died for need not end.

I hope that his story, told without sentimentality—which is how I have tried to tell it—may inspire others to carry on with the work he undertook and may help to give enduring life to the Christian gospel in places it might not otherwise have reached. Paul sometimes saw as many as 300 patients a day in our jungle hospital at Wasolo. Though he is gone, their needs continue. It is my hope, and the hope of the Carlson family, that through this book people may become deeply aware of the spiritual side of life, with its responsibilities, and will think through their personal relationship to Christ.

Lois Carlson

Torrance, California
November 1965

ACKNOWLEDGMENTS

I am indeed indebted to a great many who have encouraged and stood by me through these months. Above all to Edward Ziegler whose constant encouragement buoyed my spirits on countless occasions. To Lisa McGaw in the days of revising and editing. To Melvin Arnold, Marie Cantlon, Beverly Lancaster, Eleanor Jordan, Dorothy Pennachio, and many others at Harper & Row who have had a part in the makings of this book.

To Dr. Arden Almquist, executive secretary of world missions, and to the World Missions Board of the Evangelical Covenant Church of America for their encouragement that this book should be written. To Carl Philip Anderson, editor of Covenant Publications, for his valuable advice, counsel, and encouragement. To my pastor, Robert Honnette, for his encouragement.

To Smith, Kline & French Pharmaceuticals for the use of pictures.

To several who were with Paul while hostages who have written letters and allowed me to share them. To Congolese friends who have written to tell of events of the capture at Wasolo. To Kathryn Sundstrand for translating many letters. To our many friends and relatives who have reminisced and shared letters.

Then to our families who have been a constant source of help and encouragement. To my family who made the summer months happy ones for the children so that I was free for work on this book.

Finally, to all who have upheld us in prayer. I am forever grateful.

LOIS CARLSON

MONGANGA PAUL

I

A Call to Tandala

High atop Wasolo hill in the most obscure northeastern corner of Ubangi Province, Republic of Congo, Friday, April 10, 1964, began in a usual manner. But one thing we had learned in our short time in Congo was that no day was really like any other. Each day had its own pattern, its unexpected crisis, its surprise news on the radio.

Right after breakfast Paul had hopped on his motorbike and gone down to the hospital at the foot of the hill. Within a few minutes it would be time for the regular radio contact between our mission stations scattered throughout the Ubangi. Monitoring was one of my morning tasks, and as I tidied up after breakfast before going out to start the generator, I thought of the families like ours scattered throughout the jungle, each dependent, as we were, on the radio; each dedicated, as we were, to service as missionaries in what was, to me, a remote and unfamiliar land; each determined to bear Christian witness by example as well as by word.

Some, like Paul, were doctors. Others were evangelists, teachers, builders, nurses, technicians. We shared a common heritage as Americans and as members of the Evangelical Covenant Church of America and of the Evangelical

Free Church of America. And, in common with many members of those churches, most of us were of Scandinavian descent. Our names suggested our ties. There were other Carlsons, unrelated to us, and there were Lindquists, Edstroms, Lundblads, Thornblooms, and Berggrens. Linked with those names were place names that sounded far less familiar—Karawa, Bumba, Goyongo, and Tandala.

I went out to swing the flywheel to turn on the diesel motor in the motor house adjacent to our home. With the usual dozen or so cranks of the wheel the motor began its rhythmic pounding and the light on the generator began to glow. The power was surging through the lines, I knew, and I could go to our transmitter in Wayne's room and stand by for roll call.

Wayne, our ten-year-old son, blond, blue-eyed, always active, was at the school for missionary children in Karawa, and in his absence his room was the radio room.

On the short walk back to the house I gazed about. The day was clear and sunny—just a few puffy white clouds making the blue sky more vivid. Yes, it should be a day for clear radio transmission, I told myself. My eyes took in the view to the east. What a delightful sight! In California we would pay quite a price for a view-lot such as this. Just beyond our house the hill dropped away abruptly, giving a breathtaking view of a deep green valley stretching before us for miles. The hues of the tropical trees and foliage varied from the light greens of large-leafed banana trees to the nearly black greens of the dense hardwoods that grew there. Far in the distance could be seen the slight change in color that finally became the ribbon of the Uele River, almost visible as it wound through the rolling countryside.

No time for daydreaming, I reminded myself. I was to monitor, after all, so I quickly entered the radio room, switched on the set, and waited a moment for it to warm up. I turned on a small transistor radio, too, to make sure I didn't interrupt anyone. The transmitter's hum was audible. I depressed the button on the microphone and began to transmit:

This is Nine-Q-Three-Nine, a member of the private radio telephone network of the Mission Évangélique de l'Ubangi transmitting on the frequency of 1.297 megacycles by permission of the Democratic Republic of Congo, greeting you this morning with the following message from God's word: "The Lord is near; have no anxiety, but in everything make your requests known to God in prayer and petition with thanksgiving"—Philippians 4:6. . . . This is Nine-Q-Three-Nine calling Nine-Q-Three-One for roll call. . . . Over.

A whining hum sounded over the airwaves as a distinct voice came leaping out of the loudspeaker:

This is Nine-Q-Three-One responding to roll call. That was Gbado, the nearest station, coming in loud and clear. *This is Nine-Q-Three-One, and we have messages this morning for Three-Two and for Three-Three. . . . Over.*

There was a low moaning sound, and a blank *da-dit-da-dit-da-dit-da-dit* rapping out from some unseen telegraph key, but neither sound really interfered much that day. I depressed the button again and resumed:

This is Nine-Q-Three-Nine, Nine-Q-Three-Nine, calling Nine-Q-Three-Two for roll call. Come in, please, Nine-Q-Three-Two. . . . Over.

I released the button and waited. This would be Karawa, and we always wondered whether their batteries would recharge properly from their motor; Karawa was the only station with a transistorized transmitter, and therefore was dependent on batteries. For a moment there was a crisscross of sounds, from which a more audible whine emerged. Then a familiar voice came on:

Nine-Q-Three-Two, this is Nine-Q-Three-Two, responding to roll call. We have messages for Three-Three and Three-Eight. . . . Over.

This is Nine-Q-Three-Nine calling Nine-Q-Three-Three for roll call. Come in, Nine-Q-Three-Three. . . . Over.

I waited again. This would be Gemena, the station that had city power, which sometimes fluctuated so that transmission was impossible. I knew that Three-Two was waiting to hear what the customs regulations were on a shipment of medicines, that our mission legal representative was to find out at the government office. A solid buzzing gave way to yet another familiar voice:

This is Nine-Q-Three-Three responding to roll call. . . . We have a message for Three-Two. . . . Over.

Again I sent out a call, this time for Tandala: *This is Nine-Q-Three-Nine calling Nine-Q-Three-Four for roll call. . . . Over.*

This is Nine-Q-Three-Four, Nine-Q-Three-Four responding with messages for all stations, and Dr. Gretchen wants an after-transmission with Dr. Paul at Three-Nine.... Over.

Using the pencil and notepad I always kept at hand during transmission, I scribbled a note and called the man who provided yard help, who took it down the hill to the hospital. Gretchen and Warren Berggren were a Free Church husband-and-wife doctor team at Tandala. Apparently Gretchen had a surgical problem that she wanted to review with Paul. This kind of consultation by air was not at all unusual, so I put it out of mind. Again I was transmitting:

Nine-Q-Three-Nine calling Nine-Q-Three-Five for roll call....

The familiar voices continued—the monotone from faraway Bau, the voices from Kala, Bokada, Goyongo, and Bumba. It was always hard to hear Bumba well, even though it was directly south of us. Bumba's antenna, like ours, was beamed for messages to the west, toward Gemena, the center of the Ubangi. Still, that day, with exceptionally clear transmission, we could read even Bumba without difficulty.

The second round of station calls came then. At this time, each station gives messages, and responses to messages received. So long as the day was not stormy, which often caused a great deal of interference and fading that could slow the exchange of messages to the stopping point, the traffic could move swiftly. This day the stations, beginning with Three-One, cleared quickly. Again, it was Tandala's turn. I leaned forward to the microphone:

Calling Nine-Q-Three-Four for traffic.... Over.

Three-Four responding. Message to all stations... to all stations. We request prayer for Dr. Warren. He is very ill today. We're standing by for after-transmission with Dr. Paul.... Over.

The voice sounded very worried. We knew Dr. Warren had become ill a few days before, after spending several days with very little rest operating at one of the government hospitals. His illness, however, had been attributed to malaria. What now? I wondered. I scribbled another note to Paul.

This is Nine-Q-Three-Nine to Three-Four. Received your message. Paul will be here for immediate after-transmission....

I could feel a sense of emergency enveloping us, and so could the others, judging by the speed with which they cleared traffic. Soon I heard Paul hurrying into the house.

This is Nine-Q-Three-Nine calling Three-Four. Paul is here to talk to Gretchen, I said as Paul entered the room. I told him quickly about Warren's continuing illness. I stood up, and he glanced at the transmitter, quickly took the microphone from my hand, and slid into the chair. He leaned forward.

Go ahead, Gretchen, he said. *Go ahead. . . . Over.*

Three-Four to Three-Nine. . . . I could hear the urgency in Gretchen's voice as she explained her husband's illness to Paul in detail. This was not at all unusual, except that it involved Warren. Doctors at the various stations often conferred with each other over the radio network on methods of treatment, ways of ordering drugs, and other news of medical significance.

Paul, he's so very sick, Gretchen was saying. *In fact, early this morning he said "Goodbye" to me. I don't know what else to do by way of treatment. I need help. . . .*

I could almost see Paul wince at the words; he had felt so close to Dr. Warren since first meeting the Berggrens in 1961 when he had been in Congo for a short term. Dr. Warren, still in his thirties, had had serious stomach surgery about a year before this new crisis, when the Berggrens had been home on furlough. Now, Paul knew, with a severe illness other complications could set in.

Gretchen, do you want me to come?

Wasolo was a long way from Tandala, and we could sense Gretchen's perplexity, her reluctance to make such a request. There was silence from her end. Then it broke.

Would you?

We're on our way, Paul said.

Before these last words were out of Paul's mouth, I had moved into the bedroom to begin packing our traveling trunk. Something had told me that we would be going to Tandala. Helping me gather together the things we would need was our six-year-old daughter, Lynette. Lyn was already accustomed to the fact that, with Daddy a doctor, emergency was routine. However, her brown eyes sparkled and I knew the preparations spelled adventure to her—and no classes that day. I was teaching her first-grade subjects at home and we usually had lessons after radio call-in.

At the hospital, meantime, Jody LeVahn, the mission nurse, who had been alerted to the situation, was readying an emergency assortment of drugs to be left in the small pharmacy for the Congolese nurses' use, for she, too, would be going with us to Tandala. Jody was Paul's strong right arm at the hospital, and he counted on her to stand by in surgery or on a dash to a remote village. Since I first met Jody—her name was Joann, but I never heard her called that—in Michigan about three years before, I had associated her with Wasolo. Her alert, energetic manner and her cheerful readiness to serve always seemed to make any crisis less difficult. Jody lived in a house next to ours and we shared meals with her nearly every day.

Since these radio conversations could not be private, our other stations knew that we would be leaving Wasolo. That would mean that within about six hours—if all went well—we would come to the first station on our route, Gbado, where our cousins Frank and Margaret Lindquist were located. They were serving their third term in the Ubangi.

We would arrive at the Lindquists hungry and tired. Paul would want coffee, and they would be waiting for us. Then, within a few minutes, we would be back in the truck and jolting down the road for Karawa, a three- or four-hour run from Gbado. So it would go. People would know we were coming.

It is no simple matter to leave a bustling hospital without a doctor. The indefinite length of our absence made it no easier. How long would we be gone? A few days? A week? Two weeks? Paul returned to the hospital, and he and Jody explained to Wanzi, hospital administrator and head nurse, and to the other Congolese nurses the situation and that we did not know just when we would be back but it would be as soon as possible. In the interim, would they carry on the work there? Of course the answer was "Yes."

Meanwhile, Azupka, our cook, and I were busy getting a road lunch together; and while I continued packing, Azupka accelerated the noon-meal preparations so that we could eat early. As soon as Jody and Paul came from the hospital, we bolted down a hot meal and were off.

The weather was pleasant when we started. The roads were fairly dry, even though steering the mission truck, our means of conveyance, was difficult. This problem was not owing to the weather of the day, but to past troubles that had made the tie rods of the truck bend, which made steering a struggle for Paul. We had notified the Karawa station of our difficulties, hoping they would have a truck in better condition that they could loan us. We climbed in, waved goodbye to our Congolese friends, and went jouncing down the hill on our journey.

Paul, as usual, did not talk much when he was concentrating on driving. Also, the bumps in the roads did not permit a great deal of conversation. For the first two hours of the trip, the road was particularly bad. The potholes were such that they could not be missed. How we wished that the villagers would take the initiative to fill in some of the holes. But then they didn't have trucks so they weren't concerned. It never seemed to occur to them that if the roads were better, supplies would be more accessible to them. On any trip anywhere, Lyn usually provided entertainment in the form of singing. In France—where we had studied French before coming to Congo—it had been French songs. Now the songs were in Lingala, the Ubangi trade language. Her young voice would sustain a cheery note for us as we sped along our way as fast as the bumpy road would allow us. Our thoughts and our prayers were for Warren, and all of us were a bit gloomy.

We made it to Gbado in record time. The station mechanic swung under the truck almost as soon as it came to rest and did what he could to improve the steering. Margaret had a meal prepared for us, and this gave us a short respite. We learned that at the four o'clock radio call-in Dr. Warren was reported as holding his own. Soon we were off again. The road had been graded that day, so it was in fairly good condition for a change. One rain, however, would change it into another rutty, muddy problem.

Our next stop: Karawa. We arrived quite late—about 10 p.m.—and most of the missionaries came running out to greet us. Dr. Helen Berquist, from the hospital there, had gone to Tandala earlier in the afternoon to help. Paul was glad she had been able to get away. We inquired about trading trucks. The mechanic there, Bob Thornbloom, shook his head. "Sorry. No truck here is any better than the one you're driving. But I'll check your truck while you're having coffee and see what I can do."

Next stop: Gemena. We were thankful for a dry road, because the sandy stretches become mud and the hills become slippery slides when it rains. The Seashores had a light on in their house and some hot soup and coffee waiting for us. We bolted that down—by now it was almost 2 a.m. We had been on the road fourteen hours. A couple of hours more and we would be in Tandala. On the outskirts of Gemena the rain started to come down in torrents. We kept on.

The muddy road became a churning river, and we could no longer see the roadbed. All we could discern in the teeming scene picked out by our headlights was the muddy semblance of a river. Jody and I kept wiping the inside of the windshield to prevent it from steaming up. Outside, the windshield wipers did their best to keep the pelting raindrops cleared away. The psychological strain was intense. I became convinced that we would slide off the road. "Paul," I said at last, "please stop. We'll only go off the road. We'll get stuck. We won't get there at all."

"Lois," he replied, gravely, "I've *got* to get to Warren." He hunched lower over the steering wheel and stared into the awful darkness of what had to be the road. The rain continued to pelt down with the surprising force that only a tropical rainstorm can have. Finally, the welcome sight of Palm Lane at Tandala came into sight. Still the rain was pouring down.

So many times since then I have thought that the Lord certainly must have wanted Paul there that morning, because there was no earthly reason for us to have been able to get there. Ahead loomed the Berggren house. We could see the dim lights from the kerosene lamps radiating out toward us like welcome beacons. But we wondered what the situation was inside that house. One of the missionary nurses came running out with a raincoat and umbrella. Her face was solemn.

Paul stopped the truck with a jolt. Jumping out, he bounded up the steps and into the house. Within seconds he was at Warren's bedside. It was about 5 a.m.

Dr. Helen was with Dr. Gretchen. The three doctors prepared to confer, but first, before making any decisions, they prayed together. Then Paul put his strong arm around Gretchen's shoulders. "Go get some rest," he said. "With God's help, we'll pull him through."

Dr. Warren's pulse was thready, he had a high fever, and he hadn't slept for three days because he felt that if he did he would not wake up. Paul and Helen quickly reviewed the situation. It was clear that Warren had overwhelming pneumonia, complicated by severe malaria. A continuous intravenously administered dosage of penicillin was given, and the dim glow from the kerosene lamp cast its shadows through the room. The tenseness pervaded even the darkest corner of that sickroom. They tried another antimalarial drug, and waited to see if it would have any effect. Warren's life was hanging in the balance. As the light of the dawn came pouring in the windows and making the pale flickerings of the kerosene lanterns still paler, no one of us could imagine what the new day would bring. Paul was exhausted from a seventeen-hour drive, and Dr. Helen had been up all night. They had given Dr. Gretchen a sedative, so that she could get some rest. The night was spent, the new day was upon them, and they could only wait.

On regular radio-contact time that morning all the other stations were anxious to hear the report about Dr. Warren. The news was grave. It was decided that every two hours during this day there would be a report on Warren's condition. Later that day Paul asked for a consultation over radio with Dr. Theodora Johnson at Bokada. Dr. Teddy, as she was affectionately known, had been in Congo for many years and was well acquainted with methods of treatment for malaria. The question was, should intravenous quinine be used if the other drugs continued to have no effect? This was a risk, but as the hours wore on, and the malarial fever did not subside, it was felt that this medication had to be administered despite the risks. It was given with much prayer, and a hush fell over the station as we awaited some sign, some indication. Our concern was shared by the Congolese pastors and hospital administrator, who quietly stopped by during the course of the day.

Saturday night, Dr. Warren was slightly better. Paul and Helen said the next morning that they had each been able to take about an hour's nap during the night. Sunday, Dr. Warren seemed to rally more. The crisis at last was passing, and hearts became a little lighter, as we all offered prayers of thanks for getting

Warren through those terrible nights. However, he continued to be very weak; he was still an extremely sick man.

A decision had to be made. Was it safe for Warren to stay in the tropics when he was prone to severe malaria attacks and was in a weakened condition? Dr. Helen had gone back to her work at the Karawa hospital, Dr. Teddy was busy at Bokada, and Wasolo was waiting for Paul to return. Now Tandala, a hospital with 120 beds staffed by Drs. Warren and Gretchen, faced the prospect of no doctor on its staff. Also, the very existence of the nursing classes at Tandala depended on a doctor's supervision. The doctors had a radio consultation. The consensus was that Dr. Warren could not stay in the tropics, that his life depended on his getting home to the States. The doctors feared that Warren would not consent to leaving because he knew the great need. However, he realized his condition, and reluctantly he agreed to the decision of his colleagues.

It was a gloomy time for all. In their thoughts for future medical work in the Ubangi, Paul, Warren, and the others had been discussing plans of a far-ranging nature for the work in the area. They considered how the quality of Ubangi medicine could be improved, what innovations might be brought in, how other steps could be taken. They wrestled with the problem of a more efficient way of obtaining drugs, of the possibility of a central pharmacy, and how to institute continuing medical training. They laid plans for upgrading the two nurses' training schools, one at Tandala, the other at Karawa.

Now, they wondered, what would happen to these plans after the Berggrens' departure. So much of the planning for a central medical facility, for example, which had engaged their attention and thoughts for some months, would have to go into suspension. One plan was for a central medical facility where the nurses' training schools might become a single institution, where operating rooms and equipment and facilities could be set up in such a way that doctors from America could come out for short periods of time and be of real service to the people in Congo. Paul had a dream of such a medical unit. Strangely enough, there was a government hospital, built in the Ubangi just before Congo independence that had never been used. All the doctors were beginning to realize that possibly in the near future a vital, centralized, modern hospital could exist in the Ubangi, taking advantage of this unused structure. This was Paul's dream.

Paul felt that there was a good nucleus of personnel for such a hospital. All the missionary nurses were trained registered nurses, and some had additional specialized training. Paul had a specialty in surgery; Dr. Warren's specialty was in public health; Dr. Helen and Dr. Teddy were general practitioners; several other doctors in the United States were training in other specialties and were thinking of coming out. All this went through the minds of the doctors as they talked about Warren's departure. Still, there was no escaping the inescapable: Dr. Warren must go home.

Dr. Warren, although better, was still very weak. It was felt that he should recuperate for a week or so longer, and then as soon as his strength permitted, the Berggrens should leave for America. Gretchen asked Paul if he would accompany them as far as Leopoldville, and see that they got safely off on the long overseas flight. The flight from Gemena to Leopoldville was rather difficult, and Gretchen had a one-year-old baby, Ruthie, to take care of. She felt she needed someone to help her with Warren, should he become more weak and ill on this flight.

All these events at Tandala took place within a week of our hurried arrival. As it would still be a few days before the Berggrens left, we went back to Wasolo. Paul was eager to check on his patients. He had been within a week of catching up on his backlog of surgery cases before we went to Tandala; now he found that more had come in and once again he was far behind. He was at Wasolo just two or three days and had time to handle only the most pressing cases. Then it was time to pack his clothes for the trip to Leopoldville, and off he went again.

In the meantime, Jody, Lyn, and I stayed at Wasolo. We hoped and prayed that no cases would appear that absolutely required Paul's presence. Things went along well until one evening a woman came in who had had two previous Caesarian sections. She was clearly about to give birth again. We couldn't just let her and the baby die. And yet, what could we do? We asked ourselves, should we let Wanzi, the Congolese head nurse who had watched and helped Paul in so many operations, take a chance? Wanzi took the chance! A lovely baby girl was born alive; the mother did beautifully. Wanzi was then jokingly called *Monganga*—that is, "doctor"—by some of the villagers. Wanzi was very gracious, very humble. "The Lord helped me," he said, with a large smile on his face. This brought to my mind a similar circumstance, but a time when Paul was available.

It was on one of our first trips away from Wasolo, just after Christmas, 1963, that I really learned how far-flung was the demand on Paul's skill and how impossible it was to be free from the crying needs of the Congolese, no matter how remote the village where we might stop.

We had taken our son, Wayne, back to school at Karawa after his vacation, and were headed back to Wasolo. As usual, the truck was crammed with things. Such trips were infrequent, so when we did make a journey, we tried to do all the shopping that had to be done: our own personal things; materials for repairing our house, or Jody's, or the hospital; fabric; meat; and other things.

We made a stop at our mission dispensary in Nzale, a large river-village of many mud huts with grass roofs spread along both sides of the road with perhaps several hundred people living there. This was one of two village dispensaries supplied by the Wasolo hospital. Each dispensary had a few beds, some medicines, and other equipment; and each was staffed by one Congolese male nurse living in the village. These nurses had been trained as the mission hospital nurses had, at the Karawa hospital.

Medicines were dispensed to them regularly from the Wasolo pharmacy. The villagers were thankful to have these dispensaries where they could get a certain amount of treatment and drugs for their illnesses. Also, they were able to get some help for their women when they were having their children. The nurses there treated the most common diseases found in the Ubangi—malaria, leprosy, parasitic diseases, and general infections. The nurses would sometimes advise patients to go to the Wasolo hospital. This was no easy task for a patient, because each dispensary was about a two-hour drive from the hospital. Often the patient had no means of transportation.

Between the village and the hospital was an extremely bumpy and rutted road. We always disliked that stretch of the trip because we were tired by the time we reached it.

"This stretch always seems worse on the way home than when we start out," Paul would say to me.

"Yes," I would agree. "The potholes seem—"

"Closer together."

"And deeper and harder, when we hit them."

"The bumps are so hard my head doesn't even stay in mommy's lap," Lyn would add. She found it almost impossible to rest as she often did when sitting beside me by laying her head down in my lap.

The villagers at Nzale had heard us jouncing along and were out to greet us, standing by the road, and gathering around the truck as we got out. "*Mbote, Monganga Paul,*" they intoned. "Greetings, Dr. Paul."

"*Mbote, mbote,*" Paul said, shaking hands on all sides. The dispensary nurse rushed up to him. "*Mbote, Monganga,*" he said.

"*Mbote,* Ndikini," Paul answered. "How are you?"

"Bad trouble, *Monganga,*" Ndikini said. "A woman cannot give birth to her baby. She has been in labor for three days."

Paul strode swiftly away from the truck and across to the other side of the village into a thatched hut, accompanied by Ndikini. He bent over the woman who was lying on her low bamboo bed in obvious pain and misery. Her husband stood beside her with an anxious look on his face. His expression turned to one of hope as Paul entered. Ndikini handed Paul his stethoscope. Paul dropped to his knees and listened to the baby's heart, and then he made the quick but familiar examination. He shrugged his shoulders as he said, "We have to bring her in. Somehow we have to make room in the truck."

When I heard the decision, I knew, too, that we had to make room. But how? We didn't know where we might put even one more person, to say nothing of the relative who always came along to prepare food for the patient. The truck was only a ton-and-a-half pickup. There was a lunch box in the front, also three or four bolts of material (a Christmas gift for the women at the leper village near Wasolo from a friend in the United States).

Besides that, there was a pair of two-gallon glass demijohns that we wanted to protect from the jolts of the back part of the truck. The back of the truck was already overloaded.

The only place that we could think of to put this poor woman was in the cab with us. We stuffed the bolts of material into the middle section, and Lyn sat atop them. Her head practically bumped the top of the truck. The husband somehow found a place to crawl onto the back of the truck, and we helped the woman into the cab.

I sat next to our patient. She was in such extreme pain that we wanted to make her as comfortable as we could, which wasn't comfortable at all under the circumstances. And ahead of us was that terrible stretch of road.

Paul bent over the steering wheel to peer ahead into the approaching dusk. The villagers were gathered around looking anxiously into the truck. Ahead lay the hard, potholed road. Paul drove as fast as he could, and at the same time strained to avoid hitting bumps needlessly. If we did hit a bump hard, we would hear the familiar clattering of the truck's cargo. Occasionally, Paul would call out, "Everyone all right?"

Our patient could not speak Lingala, the African trade language we had been learning, so only the tone of our expressions of concern and our gestures could reassure her.

Each bump we hit made the poor woman wince. She would have a very hard labor pain and grit her teeth while trying to keep her discomfort to herself. Meanwhile, I was watching her to see if we might have to stop along the roadside and deliver the baby. Paul would glance at me from time to time to see what my expression told him, and then he would turn his eyes back to the narrow dirt road and seem to bear down himself, as if by concentration the miles before us would melt away.

"I don't know if we're going to make it, Paul," I said.

"Just let me know when I should stop," he said.

The minutes dragged by. Finally I could tell we were getting close to Wasolo. It had been an hour and a quarter—instead of the usual two hours—I could see by my watch, and suddenly there was the reassuring WASOLO sign and the welcome sight of the cream-colored hospital.

We drove up to the middle building at the hospital and called for someone to bring the stretcher. The nurses helped Paul and me get the woman into the operating room, where Paul checked her. The baby's heartbeat was still strong and the mother was in good condition, although very tired. Paul established that a Caesarean section was absolutely necessary if this baby was to stand a chance of surviving. The woman's husband was very worried, naturally, yet now that we had reached Wasolo he seemed to be relieved at the same time. There were several minutes to spare, Paul determined. That would give him time to grab a bite to eat and wash up before surgery began.

While the nurses were preparing for the operation we went up the hill to our house. It was dusk by this time. Paul was very hungry, tired, and sweaty from the all-day trip—and from the strain of the last two hours, especially. He was silent, as was usual when he was tired and had much on his mind.

We quickly had a bite to eat, which Jody had already prepared for us, anticipating our return. Paul ate rapidly and wordlessly, and then hurried down to the hospital with Jody. When they got there everything was in readiness to perform the operation. But it was dark by this time, and the problem of the hospital's light plant was still haunting us. The plant seldom worked well, and sometimes it did not work at all. It was a difficult plant to get started, but that night they did get it going.

When Paul delivered the baby—a boy—it was very reluctant to breathe. Jody mouth-breathed it, even though she had a cold at the time, and soon the baby began breathing properly. The mother came through the operation nicely, too, and Paul was very happy. He knew that if he had not chanced by Nzale that day another mother and child would have died.

A few days later the baby developed a bad cold, but with some penicillin and a little extra care, he recovered. The mother went home in just a week, and her trip home was also by truck. Paul had an errand in that village, and she and her husband went along with him. We stopped there on our next trip and found the baby thriving. His parents had named him "Wasolo," after our mission station.

Crisis, I had learned, was routine at Wasolo.

Many incidents come flooding back as I look over our photographs and reread the letters that we wrote home and the scraps of diary that I kept. How often Paul had remarked that we would never have any trouble thinking of things to write home about!

Frequently I reflect on what happens to the multitudes without medical help. What happens to other women and other babies like Wasolo? In the United States we have many doctors, and still we have to wait for an appointment. In Congo there are no appointments. Many people walk for days when in need of care. The closest doctor to Wasolo, when there was a doctor on the hospital staff, was six truck-hours away—and trucks are infrequent and usually filled.

Paul had seen these great needs during a short term in 1961 just after Congo's independence. My thoughts turn back to events that led to our going to the heart of Africa.

II

A Pattern Forming

P aul's father could see three clocks at the instant of Paul's birth. One showed two minutes to midnight, another midnight, and a third two minutes after midnight.

"How do you want the birth certificate to read, Mr. Carlson?" the doctor asked. "March 31 or April 1?"

"I don't want him to be an April Fool's baby," Gust Carlson said, "so let's call it March 31." The year was 1928 and the place Culver City, California.

Paul's father, Gust Carlson, from a family of skilled craftsman, had come to America from Sweden at the age of ten with his parents and his thirteen brothers and sisters. The family settled in Rockford, Illinois, where Gust finished his schooling and began work as a machinist, in the family tradition. The cold rains of Rockford were still in his memory when he first saw Los Angeles with the bright sun streaming down from a clear blue sky and the fresh breezes from the Pacific. He knew right away that California was the place for him. Then he went west permanently with his bride, Ruth, also of Swedish descent, and continued to work as a machinist.

Not long after that Paul was born. Five years later, another son, Dwight, was born, and the family was completed with the birth of Sharon in 1941. Within a short time after the birth of each child, each baby was brought to church by Ruth and Gust and was dedicated to the Lord with the prayer that each life would be used of the Lord. The parents' prayer at that time was that they would have the wisdom to direct and teach their children in the way that they should go.

During his earliest years Paul suffered from asthma and preferred being read to and later reading for himself than participating in strenuous play. Paul was an able and dedicated student, always systematic about studying. He had a definite time of day for it, and he drilled himself laboriously and at great length until he had mastered the assignment.

Though serious about his studies, Paul also participated in the usual brotherly escapades. Among them was one very vivid in Dwight's mind. Dwight had purchased a motorcycle even though his parents had not exactly approved. Paul was very interested and enthused over Dwight's purchase and wanted to try it out. Dwight explained the controls and Paul set out down a dead-end street for a trial jaunt. He wound up jumping the curb and became pinned under the cycle on a neighbor's newly watered lawn. His leg was injured but not broken. Though in pain he concealed his limp in front of his parents because the boys feared that if the folks found out about the accident they would make Dwight sell the motorcycle.

The Carlson family was always close-knit, and their family affections were cemented by the strong faith of the parents. Each day, for instance, before the children left for school, they paused with their mother at the front door for a brief prayer. Gust Carlson spent long hours at his machine shop but often on Sunday afternoons after morning church service the family would go to Laguna Beach for a picnic and the children would enjoy the ocean breakers and climbing on the jagged rocks. Occasional vacations were at Crestline in the nearby San Bernardino Mountains. They enjoyed the beauty and quiet and swimming in the clear mountain lake.

Just as I recognize the Paul I knew in the stories his parents would tell of his early years, so I recognize him in the account of his enthusiasm and initiative in church work, which always filled a central part in his life. First Covenant

Church of Los Angeles had an active youth program that owed much of its drive and sparkle to "Coach" (Clarence) and Florence Johnson. Coach had been a professional baseball player and was now a surveyor with the city. These activities made the teenage years particularly full and fruitful for the thirty-odd boys and girls who formed the nucleus of the church's Hi-Y League.

Paul served as president of the group for two years, and through its work his spiritual life deepened at the same time that he learned a great deal about working with people. He always looked back on those years as among the happiest and most formative of his life. The group went on picnics, engaged in Bible study, held retreats, issued its own newspaper, had its own banquets, its own sports events. Many of those members are today pastors, pastors' wives, missionaries, teachers, Sunday-school superintendents—all continuing to lead lives as strong and faithful Christians.

Ruth Carlson recalled the problem of feeding a hungry crowd of teenagers in those days. The Second World War was in progress then, and food was rationed. "Every Sunday afternoon, when the Hi-League had its meetings, they had to have something to eat. When they met at our house, we bought bologna sausage and we ground it, and then, to make it go further, we mixed it with hard-boiled eggs and mayonnaise and made sandwiches. The kids loved it, and they didn't know how we struggled to get something for them to eat. We would have to use some of our own ration tickets so we could give them food."

Paul, meantime, as his friend Rolph Peterson remembered him, played a key role in making the Hi-League the vital organization it was. "Paul always joined in the moods of the group," Rolph said. "He had the ability to enter into other people's feelings. He struck me as a quiet type, but as I began to know him, he was really quite confident, especially with the girls at this time, because he was probably a little more mature than the average fellow his age in the Los Angeles church then."

Coach Johnson remembered the initiative Paul displayed on behalf of the church during the war. "It was Paul's idea to go out and invite servicemen to our church." Paul took a group of Hi-Leaguers to a busy intersection in Los Angeles, where they handed out cards to servicemen that told them how they could reach First Covenant Church, what time regular services were, and of other activities and social events. The church social hall was equipped with sleeping facilities for servicemen to spend weekend nights when they had passes.

One of Paul's friends, Raymond Lindberg, recalled, "I first met Paul at Alhambra High School, and through him I joined the Hi-Y. Once Paul and I went to Long Beach to hear a missionary speaker who had impressed Paul at various meetings around the Los Angeles area. During this meeting Paul dedicated his life to the mission field. When the call went out to those who felt they wanted to decide, Paul went forward.

"He was a happy kind of person, but he had a serious side, too. I think this is borne out by the fact that he finished a four-year high school course in just three years and that he was a member of the Scholarship Society." Ray added, "Paul always had in the back of his mind to be first a doctor and then to go to the mission field as a doctor."

Rolph also recalled Paul's interest in medicine. As early as 1941, at a church camp at Forest Home, California, Paul and Rolph were staying in a cabin whose counselor was a medical student. "Paul had a great admiration for this student because of the fact that he was studying medicine. Just the fact that he was putting forth this type of effort seemed to impress Paul greatly, and I believe that at this time Paul was thinking in the back of his mind that this would be a profession to follow."

In the fall of 1945, Paul entered the University of California at Los Angeles; but he found it large and impersonal, not the kind of school he felt he needed, so he left after one semester, planning then to enter the Navy. Rolph also planned to go into the Navy soon, and the two of them decided on one last adventure before enlisting—a hitchhiking trip from California to Michigan, where Paul's aunt and uncle lived, and back to California. The adventure took a month.

Soon afterward, Rolph and, a few months later, Paul, joined the Navy. Paul's two-year hitch, coming at the end of the war, was not strenuous. Following it he resumed his college education, this time in Chicago.

In a New Testament, which Paul gave a friend during his late teenage years, he had copied a poem; neither title nor author was included:*

I slept, I dreamed, I seemed
To climb a hard ascending track,
And just behind me labored one
Whose skin was black.

I pitied him, but hour by hour
He gained upon my path.
He stood beside me; stood upright
And then I turned in wrath.

"Go back," I cried, "What right
Have you to stand beside me here?"
I paused, struck dumb with fear,
For lo, the black man was not there,
But Christ stood in his place.
And oh! the pain, the pain, the pain,
That looked from that dear face.

I had entered the School of Nursing at Swedish Covenant Hospital in Chicago in September 1947, and in February 1948 I received my cap, a coveted honor. It was soon after the capping ceremony that I first met Paul.

Several of us girls were busy at work in the utility room of the hospital on the third floor, north, when the evening supervisor came into the room with a young man.

"Girls," she said, "this is Paul Carlson. He's studying at North Park College, and he's coming to help as orderly in the evenings from five to nine." Turning to Paul, she added, "You'll be getting to know these girls quite well."

"Yes, he sure will!" I exclaimed. It was a very busy floor so an orderly meant welcome help for us student nurses. He just gave me a big smile and left to see more of the ward.

I soon formed a high opinion of Paul Carlson. He was unfailingly pleasant and helpful. He never seemed to have bad moods or to be impatient when one

---

*The verses are adapted from the poem "Christ Crucified" by Ella Wheeler Wilcox.

of us asked for his help. He was willing to give us a hand with hard tasks, such as lifting a heavy patient into bed, cleaning up, or any other demanding work.

One day, as I was washing a basin at the old black-marbled sink in the utility room, I heard the swinging door pop open and a voice say, "Lois?"

"Oh, hello, Paul," I said, turning toward him.

"Lois, do you play tennis?"

"I've batted a ball around," I said, "but I don't exactly play tennis."

"Well, would you like to play tennis tomorrow in River Park?" The park was close by and was one of the loveliest places around. I turned his question over in my mind, but not for long.

"Sure," I said. I had to scramble around to borrow a racket. As it turned out, snow fell that day, so the outdoor tennis game became indoor ping-pong. I can't say that I was sorry to miss tennis.

After a few weeks I was transferred to another ward in normal rotation, but Paul stayed on Three-North, the men's ward. We didn't work together after that. We went out several times that spring, and I was dating others, as well. There was something about Paul that seemed special though, and by late fall 1948 we were dating steadily, and beginning to think about the future. Paul had at least three more years of college plus four years of medical school.

"I just don't know if it's fair for us to talk about spending our lives together, Lois, when I have such a long period of schooling. It would mean so much work for you for so many years, right at the start." He talked in terms of the mission field once his schooling was completed. I told him that early in my teens I, too, had felt that I would be willing to go into missionary work.

We seemed to agree in our approach to our faith. Neither one of us felt an absolutely compelling and overwhelming force that commanded us only to the mission field and to no other service. Both of us felt that we ought to prepare for several possibilities, and to try to avoid any rigid preconceptions about where life would carry us.

Variations of this conversation took place time and again, and we never did come to a single day when we could say, "This is it." Rather, it built up slowly. One day, I remember, we discussed this question again in what we called the "beau parlor" in the new nurses' dormitory at Swedish Covenant Hospital.

We had come in from a Youth for Christ rally. With a few minutes before curfew, we went through it again. Within me were many thoughts that I could not actually voice. I could sense that being with Paul would doubtless mean going into mission work of some sort—in America or overseas. At that time in my life, though, I wasn't highly enthusiastic about mission work.

I could see the man in whom I was very interested suggesting that our life together would begin in struggle and continue in uncertainty—and yet I knew I didn't want to let him go. Because of our belief in prayer and in the Lord's direction of our lives, we prayed about our dilemma. In my heart, I continued to hope that God would not find use for me as a missionary. I wanted a calmer, more orderly kind of life. I wasn't bent on adventure. I think I knew by then that if I said "yes" to Paul I was probably saying "yes" to the mission field as the wife of a medical missionary.

This was my state of mind at the time Paul left for California to spend the Christmas holidays with his parents. I had no vacation then, but it was an exciting time of year at the hospital, because of the festive decorations, the caroling, and the warm hospitality that pervades a Swedish Christmas. Yet as I went about my regular duties, a sense of loneliness and turmoil filled me.

Christmas morning came, and before daylight, by tradition, our "big sisters" served us breakfast in bed. I was awakened by an orange landing on me: they didn't serve breakfast very gracefully! After that, I went to early chapel, and then a group of us walked up and down the dark corridors of the hospital, carrying lighted candles, dressed in our blue-and-white-striped uniforms with starched aprons and white caps, and sang carols until we had to go on duty at 7 a.m.

The days dragged on, and the last day of December finally came. Paul arrived during the afternoon, and in the evening—New Year's Eve—we drove with another couple into the northern suburbs of Chicago to an area famous for its Christmas decorations. As we stopped at one house with a particularly beautiful display, the other couple decided that they wanted to see it close up, and they jumped out of the car. During those few moments, while they were looking at the decorations, Paul asked me if I would marry him.

"Yes," I replied without hesitation. After all the discussions and inner anxiety, the decision came quickly and firmly, with no doubt on my part.

"What's the matter with you two?" asked our friends as they got back into the car.

"Oh, we've got a secret." And that was all we said.

We had agreed not to make our engagement public until summer because I still had one and a half years of my course to complete. I saw no more of Paul after that than I had before, because in addition to his studies, he was very active in extra-curricular activities. He was president of the Demenudi Club, a society of those studying at North Park to be doctors, nurses, dentists, and dieticians. He was also active on the yearbook staff.

Our engagement was announced at a party at my parents' home in Menominee, Michigan, on the Fourth of July weekend 1949. Paul went to summer school at North Park, and in August he received his Associate of Arts degree. We parted in September, when he returned to California to enter Stanford University as a junior. I went to Children's Memorial Hospital in Chicago for my training in pediatrics, and the transition to a new assignment made his absence less painful. Paul, in the meantime, was quickly establishing himself in the life at Stanford, and we were both eagerly looking forward to our wedding day.

We were married on the evening of September 16, 1950, at the Evangelical Covenant Church in Menominee, and our families and relatives were all around us. I had just met Paul's parents, who had made the trip from Los Angeles only four days before the wedding.

We got away just for the weekend, and on the following Wednesday and Thursday I had to be in Chicago to take my Illinois State Board examinations for my nurse's license. I had completed my training only five weeks before the wedding. The evening before my exam, Paul had gone to Detroit to pick up a new car, which he had agreed to drive to the West Coast for its owner. We had to be at Stanford in time for him to start his senior year there.

So, four days after our wedding, my husband was in Detroit picking up the car that would take us west, and I was in Chicago struggling with a rigorous two-day examination covering all phases of nursing: surgery, medicine, obstetrics, pediatrics, and psychiatry. The evening after the examination, Paul picked me up. We had only until the following Tuesday to drive to Stanford, the final day of registration there. I began to brood over the results of my test.

"I wonder if I'll have to go back."

"Where?"

"Chicago."

"Why?"

"Well, the test. I wonder if I passed it."

"Oh, sure you passed it. Just don't worry about it," he said.

We repeated that conversation a number of times, and Paul's unfailing optimism buoyed me whenever I became glum about the test.

When we arrived in Atherton, near Stanford, Paul had a surprise for me. He had found a small cottage for us on an estate where he agreed to do one day's work a week as gardener in return for the cottage at a modest rental. It was a quaint place set among shrubbery. Growing up the side of the house and onto the roof was a rosebush which was in bloom and scenting the dooryard with its delicate fragrance. Paul's gardening tasks were largely confined to Saturdays and he spent the evenings studying.

After taking six weeks off, I had to get a job. I had passed my exams after all, and my certification was in order. That made it possible to apply for California registration, and soon I was at work at Menlo Medical Center.

Meanwhile, both Paul and I were caught up in Stanford campus life—he because of his day-by-day involvement, and I because the community was so interested in the college activities. We rarely missed a Stanford home football game. Paul was an ardent rooter and often came home with little voice remaining after a particularly close game. Though he had never taken an active part in football or baseball, his interest in these sports ran high.

Paul was active in the InterVarsity Christian Fellowship. One day the university chaplain, Robert Minto, asked Paul if he could arrange to have a Sunday school at the Stanford Convalescent Home (for children) in Palo Alto. Four or five of us, under Paul's leadership, developed a program for the "Con Home," as we called it.

It was a challenge to Paul and a thrill to both of us to see what the work meant to the children. As we came in sight on Sunday, the youngsters—usu-

25

ally about sixty in number—would commence to chant: "Here comes Sunday school, here comes Sunday school," with obvious delight. Since we worked with children of every faith, Paul reasoned that we should present basic Bible stories and sing simple hymns that would not be objectionable to people of divergent religious backgrounds. He was determined that we teach them without religious clichés. We faced a stern test when the parents of the children visited them, because the youngsters always described what they had learned in Sunday school that week.

To keep a direct, simple approach required hard work on our part. We tried to avoid the stereotyped church language that so often closes people's ears to the message of Christ. Many of the children had no strong church background, and some had never heard any of the Bible stories before. I still chuckle when I remember the small Chinese boy, one of our most earnest and attentive students, who recited the Lord's Prayer at bedtime: "... deliver us from eagles," he prayed.

Paul believed firmly that a living witness accomplished more in some circumstances than the preaching approach. As we prepared the lessons, we analyzed our own childhood teachings, examined our own faith closely, and asked ourselves what that faith really meant in our personal lives. It was this preparation, I think, that helped make ready the way for our eventual Congo service. This was my first experience in working with Paul in such a situation, and his awareness of the problems of telling the good news of the Bible so that the message was not lost in the verbiage opened my eyes to the kind of ministry he foresaw for himself.

During this year, Paul began applying to medical schools. There was a great influx of G.I.'s then, and medical schools were overflowing. One by one, the replies came. Classes were filled.

Our finances were rather low. My salary wasn't enough to support us completely, so Paul took a night orderly job in the psychiatric unit of the Veterans Administration Hospital. It was at this point that he would be arriving home from his night job just as I was leaving for my daytime job, and that was a curious arrangement.

In June 1951 Paul received his Bachelor of Science degree from Stanford, with a major in anthropology. He decided he would forge ahead, despite his disappointments, and take work on his master's degree in anthropology the following year. Paul was not going to let his momentary lack of success get him down. Again, during the year of graduate work, the applications to medical school went out. Again we waited. Then, one day, as Paul came down the driveway from the mailbox, I could see in his face the signs of joy. I knew in my heart that the news was good.

"Lois! An acceptance!" he said excitedly, and we almost danced for joy. Then, as so often happens at times like those, a second acceptance came within a few days. Now we faced the question, "Which one do we pick?" But the decision was not difficult. Among the acceptances was one from Paul's first choice of schools, the George Washington University School of Medicine in Washington, D.C.

How would we move ourselves 3,000 miles east? That was our next problem. Although we had no furniture to speak of, we did have personal belongings, including Paul's ever increasing library of books. Paul found a solution, of course, and in due time we were on our way east in a secondhand, homemade trailer, which Paul had proceeded to remodel after purchasing. When we arrived in Washington in 1952, apartments were very scarce.

"Sorry, no vacancies and none likely," was all we heard. Finally, we saw an advertisement in a newspaper, and we were sitting on the steps of the agent's office the next morning before he came to work.

"Sorry," he said, "I've got a list of about twenty applicants waiting for that apartment."

Paul said in his earnest way, "But I'm attending medical school and classes start in a week."

"Twenty people..."

"We came all the way from California," Paul said.

The agent relented. He let us see the apartment.

"You're supposed to have a place of employment," the agent said.

Somehow all the obstacles were overcome and we moved our few possessions in. For some time, trunks were our chairs, the ironing board our dining room table, and a mattress on the floor our bed. As time went on, we acquired furniture piece by piece. I remember one little girl coming down from an upstairs apartment and saying, "Oh, you *have* furniture in your apartment!" She had heard the other children asking us, "When's the moving van coming?"

During the first fall, when the study was very intensive for Paul, I was nursing at Walter Reed Army Medical Center, first on alternating shifts and then on night duty. The night shift seemed to be the lesser of two evils because I could sleep while Paul was in school, and then get up in time to prepare dinner, so we could have the evening together. With my income and the money that Paul had through the G.I. Bill, we managed, but with nothing to spare.

During this time we attended Wallace Memorial Presbyterian Church because there was no Covenant church in Washington. We also became active in the chapter of the Christian Medical Society at George Washington. The members—doctors, and medical students—sought to further the application of Christian principles in medicine, and in medical missions also. Their belief in spreading the gospel message, a prominent feature of the society, was one of the things that attracted Paul to it.

When Paul was a senior, he became president of the chapter. During his time with the society, they set up a one-night-a-week medical clinic at the Gospel Mission in Washington. Here homeless would come for a hot meal and a bed, and could hear a gospel message. Many of them were ill, and the medical students belonging to the Christian Medical Society took turns at the clinic.

In addition to his work at the mission medical clinic, Paul was instrumental in inviting medical students at Howard University College of Medicine, a historically black school, to the functions of George Washington's Christian Medical Society chapter, and in this way helped them to establish a chapter at their school.

Paul was elected to the Kane-King obstetrical and the Smith-Reed-Russell honor societies, both indications of how able a student he was. Along with his bent for studying and getting good grades, he enjoyed a good time. He always took an active part in the medical school "Follies."

In the spring of Paul's junior year—on March 16, 1955—our first child,

Wayne, was born. I returned to work the summer after his birth, and my younger sister came east from Michigan to care for him until fall. The last year, rather than going out to work, I looked after two small babies of friends of ours, keeping them on a day-care basis in our apartment.

Paul, meantime, took a part-time job in the emergency and operating rooms of one of the city hospitals. Again, it was the familiar merry-go-round of work and school and more work.

Paul kept very busy his senior year, yet he was happy because he was at last doing clinical work, working with the patients right in the hospital. That year the decision had to be made about internship—where he would go and what training he would take after that. At Christmastime we made our only trip to Los Angeles during the four years of medical school. The main purpose of the trip, besides seeing family, was for Paul to examine the various programs for internship and surgical residency in the hospitals in the Los Angeles area. He chose surgery, again with the possibility of missionary work in mind. He felt that on the mission field surgery was, above all other medical specialties, the most useful.

In June 1956 Paul was awarded his M.D. degree with distinction. It was a very happy day in our lives. We knew that years of training still lay ahead, but the hardest part was behind us.

A new phase of our life began with Paul interning at the hospital of his choice—Harbor General in Torrance, California. Now we were near Paul's boyhood home, and within an hour's drive of where his parents were living. If all went well, he could look forward to a year of internship, followed by a four-year residency in surgery.

Paul had chosen Harbor General Hospital because it offered a rotating internship and a residency program in the field in which he wished to special-ize. As the years went on, and as the continual weight of responsibility and duty pressed down on him and on us, the quality of our life changed for a time, and it caused us worry and concern. We passed through a long and try-ing period, that now, when I look back on it, is best described as "the difficult years."

At first we lived in an apartment, but soon we made a down payment (with a loan from Paul's parents) on a small house just being built near the hospital. When I look back on it, I realize what a bold step we took, because if Paul had not received an appointment to a surgical residency at Harbor the next year, we would have had to pull up stakes and sell the house.

I intended to clean house before we moved in, but one night, on the spur of the moment, I telephoned Paul as he was finishing duty. "Do you suppose we could go over and get the key for the house so we can move in tomorrow?"

"What's got into you?"

"I just can't stand it in this apartment. . . . Wayne has no freedom for play."

"Sure," he said. "Let's go get it."

We got the key that evening, and moved in the next day, with Gust's help, right into the sawdust and wood chips, the fragments of molding and the dust left by the construction workers. It was a matter of only a few blocks and a rented trailer, so this was the easiest move we had made during our married life and it seemed almost unbelievable to us that we were moving into a place that we could call our own—a mortgaged home, but we felt it was more ours than anything else we had lived in.

Wayne, of course, was overjoyed to have a place in which to run around and play. For a while it was muddy play because the yard wasn't completed, but that was all the more incentive for us to put it in order. In the evenings and afternoons, when Paul was relatively free, he leveled off the lot, shovelful by shovelful, built a retaining wall, and fixed up our lawn. He took great pride in planting flowers. Whenever we visited friends who had particularly pretty flowers in the yard, he would ask with a small grin, "Don't some of these need thinning out a bit?" We couldn't afford to go to the nursery and buy plants, so our yard displayed quite an array of flowers from other people's gardens.

Having a home of our own meant that we could have the family in for birthdays, Sunday gatherings, and other celebrations. Paul never forgot birthdays or holidays.

Paul enjoyed helping to fix up the inside of the house, too. He always had ideas about the placement of furniture, what kind of pictures to have on the walls, and he had a keen sense of color. I kidded him more than once that he had missed his calling; he should have been an interior decorator. He would laugh and say in his direct and disarming way, "Well, I enjoy this kind of thing." I told him that for his taste we needed a thicker pocketbook; but we hit on a good compromise in furnishing our house, and eventually we had a very cozy home that we greatly enjoyed.

Paul was accepted for his surgical residency at Harbor General and we looked forward to the completion of his internship and his licensing in California. With Paul very busy in his hospital work, I continued to work full time as a night nurse and to take care of Wayne in the daytime. By this time, with Paul's licensing on the horizon, our second baby was on the way. Our daughter, Lynette, was born October 20, 1957.

A few days before her arrival, Paul received his license to practice medicine in California. That made it possible for me to quit my nursing job. He got a part-time job at the Redondo Beach Medical Clinic, which brought in the extra paycheck that we so needed to get along.

This continued to be a rugged and hectic schedule. The evenings that he worked at the clinic, he would rush home for a bite of dinner, throw on a clean shirt, dash out the door to the car, and hurry down to the clinic. Occasionally he filled in on other part-time jobs that came along. This was the regular routine of residents at that time, because the pay from the hospital was too low to support a family. Also, as part of the residency program, he was on duty about every third night on an all-night call basis.

This schedule tended to put Paul under severe pressure. During this period he had very little time for any church activities. When we first moved to Torrance, we often saw a group of young couples, most of whom had come from the downtown First Covenant Church of Los Angeles, which Paul had attended in his boyhood. Some of these couples had also been there as youngsters. They were interested in organizing a church in the Rolling Hills–Torrance area, because it was hard to get into downtown Los Angeles. On Wednesday evenings, we would get together with them for Bible study and prayer, but as Paul was extremely busy during residency, and the children were still very young, we found it difficult to have time to get out with the group.

The subject of medical missions was mentioned less and less during this period. Eventually it disappeared completely from our discussions. One reason for our lagging interest was because we knew our own denomination was not sending additional doctors to the field. Medical mission work is expensive, and medicine was not being stressed or increased in the mission program at that time. The possibility of our being called seemed remote. Neither of us felt the call to the mission field great enough to warrant our inquiring of other denominational mission boards about being sent out. Few people among Paul's new medical colleagues realized that in his background had been the desire to be a medical missionary. If the subject of medical missions did come up, some were apt to scoff, and Paul did not encourage conversation along these lines.

Paul became very confused, a man in turmoil and stress. In the day-by-day struggles, the contest of life and death at the hospital, and the discussions that followed different turns of events, it seemed that there was a question in Paul's mind, as well as in the minds of some of his colleagues, of the very existence of a Triune God, the existence of One who does guide and shape our beings and lives. It was sometimes difficult for him to express his feelings in thoughts and words, which made it difficult for me, too, because I knew that he was going through a perplexing time. I wanted so much to help, and still I hardly knew how to cope with it. But here, turning to God in prayer was the source of strength that I needed. In praying for Paul when I could not always talk to him directly about things that were bothering him, I found strength.

Paul continued his real interest in things that went on around the house, in fixing things up, entertaining our friends, visiting with neighbors, playing with the children, and assuming the roles of father and householder, neighbor and doctor, much as any other man might have done.

He wanted to have the whole surgical staff of the Harbor General Hospital, including the chief of surgery, to a Swedish smörgåsbord. New Year's afternoon of the second year of residency turned out to be the day. A smörgåsbord requires so many foods that it takes a great deal of planning to know where to put the dishes and the silverware on the table, where to put the food, and where to put the beverages. Paul was always the one to solve such matters. The party was scheduled for 6 p.m., and at 4 p.m., as I began to clean up the stacks of dishes used in the day-long task of preparing the food, we had a sudden crisis: the garbage disposal clogged. Paul dashed next door to borrow a snake to clean out the drain. It didn't work. Then a couple of neighbors offered assistance, to no avail. Paul even tried to bribe the hospital plumber from his home, because the whole surgical department was coming. That didn't work, either. No plumber wanted to come out on New Year's Day.

"Well, just act as if nothing has happened," Paul finally said.

"How can I?"

"Try."

"But I don't want people to think that this is the way I keep my kitchen!"

The sink was two-thirds full of water, with all the garbage that did not go down the disposal unit floating in it. The pots and pans were stacked as high as they could be without toppling over. And I was to act as if all were normal!

"I can't just go on as if nothing has happened," I insisted.

Paul and our dear neighbor came to my rescue. My neighbor took some of the pots and pans home to wash and Paul found a big box in the garage, and that is where he packed the other dirty pans for the duration of the party. We proceeded to scoop the water and the garbage out of the sink, and in a little while, it looked as if nothing were amiss.

The first guests to arrive, the chief of surgery and his wife, soon gravitated to the kitchen area and others followed, as I knew they would, since our house had an open floor plan. The table was laden with cheeses of several kinds, lingonberry sauce, pickled herring, *limpa* (Swedish rye bread), rolls, two or three molded fruit and vegetable salads, carrot pudding, small parsley potatoes, Swedish meatballs, ham, and *potatis korv* (a sausage made of beef, pork, and potato). We had the traditional rice pudding for dessert, and of course coffee, cookies, Swedish coffee breads, and more coffee. It was a festive party and a great success.

Still interwoven with these happy occasions was the turmoil that continued in Paul's mind. He would seem to relax completely at times, but at other times it would come back strongly, and I knew the inner struggle was continuing as the end of his residency approached. Everyone was growing excited about where each one would go into practice, what opportunities there were in different areas, the pros and cons of various cities and towns, the best places to live, and similar questions.

There was a lot of discussion about how much it cost to go into practice, from the standpoint of renting an office and then equipping it not only with furniture but with all the diagnostic equipment that is needed. This seemed to run into staggering amounts of money. Then there was the question of whether one's office would be close enough to a hospital or other facility where there was x-ray equipment or whether it would be necessary to buy that, too. In all, it seemed to be a crushing amount of overhead in private practice.

In group practice, equipment costs could be shared, but then there was the worry of personalities working together. "Is this the kind of partner I want to go in with?" would be the question vexing them next. Each of these perplexing problems had to be weighed, analyzed, and answered. In such analysis, more than one of Paul's colleagues, as well as Paul, would think he had found an ideal situation, only to discover at the last moment that there was something wrong—a bad office arrangement, a disagreeable personality trait of a prospective partner, or some other problem. Then the talk would turn again to expenses, to the possibilities of borrowing from banks or equipment manufacturers. There was the question of how much they would have to go into debt, above and beyond whatever debts they carried at the end of a twelve-year training period.

One of the wives, whose husband was in his first year of practice, said, "You don't know how good you've got it now. At least you've got that resident's check coming in each month."

At the beginning of 1961, the year when Paul would finish, a letter came from the Christian Medical Society with an "Operation Doctor" appeal from the Congo Protestant Relief Agency. They were asking doctors in the United States to go to Congo on a short-term basis to relieve the shortage of medical personnel which then was particularly acute. The Republic of Congo had been granted independence by Belgium just six months earlier. In the unrest that ensued, many Belgian and other European doctors had fled the country, leaving both government hospitals and mission hospitals unstaffed. The appeal was for one-year volunteers. Their fare would be paid and they would be given a small stipend.

This appeal brought the possibility of medical mission work to the fore again, and Paul and I discussed it. I have to admit that I wasn't eager to become involved in this kind of work because, as the months rolled along, and as the doctors and their wives we knew talked about the future, we felt ourselves on the verge of going into practice, and we were anticipating a better income after years of struggle. By this time in Paul's training we were doing reasonably well financially, and we were beginning to taste the comforts that American life offers.

In the early spring, another letter came from the Christian Medical Society office, with a further appeal for short-term workers in Congo, again under the Congo Protestant Relief Agency. This time the term was four months, or longer.

As I opened and read the letter, it struck me that here was something that Paul would want to know more about. He had said when the first appeal came that he wouldn't consider leaving his family for an entire year. That would be too long. The matter had been set aside again, and I was pleased that that was the close of that episode. But a four-month term—I knew he would think seriously about a short period.

This second letter came at a time when Paul was on duty for several days in a row, and the stack of mail that he was to look at when he came home grew quite high. I couldn't bring myself to throw the letter away, but I did put it at the bottom of the pile, thinking that he wouldn't find time to get at it until it was too late.

Paul got to the letter. He was very interested, as I thought he would be.

"Lo, I feel this is something I should inquire into and find out more about."

"I see."

"Do you think it would be unreasonable to think in terms of going for a four-month period?"

I knew I couldn't hold him back, so I said, rather reluctantly, "Well, find out more about it, if you want to."

Then came another period of a few days when he was gone, and I was opening the mail again. It was early June, and when I saw the envelope from the Christian Medical Society, I expected a further explanation of Operation Doctor. Instead of additional information, the letter asked Paul to go, and even gave him an overseas flight date—July 18. I felt devastated.

"What does this mean?" I asked as soon as Paul came home. "Everything seems all set. But you didn't even tell me you'd written a letter."

"I'm sorry, Lois. I found time one evening at the clinic to get a letter off. I forgot to tell you I had mailed it." He looked at me for a moment. "I had no idea any answer would come this fast," he said, and I could see that he was surprised, too.

Through the period that led up to this day, I had sensed a real change of heart and attitude in Paul. This made me feel better about things, although the thought of his going overseas for a while into a place that was in political turmoil was not appealing. Still, I knew that I shouldn't and couldn't stop him because, as he said, "You know, Lois, I've always thought in terms of medical missionary work, and I firmly believe that this is my answer, that the Lord is showing me that this is something he wants me to do. I feel that I should do it."

"All right, Paul," I said. "We'll manage, and the time will pass quickly."

I I I

Operation Doctor

At a church-sponsored steak-fry one evening early in July, when everyone introduced themselves and said what kind of work they did, Paul and I disclosed our plans. Paul and I rose and faced the group.

"Paul and Lois Carlson," he said. "I'm a doctor and I'm going to do mission work in Congo for several months beginning this July 18." There was a gasp from the group, because even our closest friends had not heard of Paul's decision to go.

Day by day our preparations continued—Paul securing his passport and other documents he would need; I preparing to take the children to Michigan, where we would spend the summer with my parents.

Quickly July 18 arrived. By then we were all in Michigan and we took Paul to O'Hare Airport in Chicago for the flight for Leopoldville. It was a day of mixed emotions for us. Of course Paul was happy to be going, to be doing something that in his heart he had always wanted to do. On the other hand, it was difficult for him to part with his family and for all of us to part with him. But we girded ourselves for a period of separation, and with a cheery wave, he was out through the gate and onto the plane.

Paul stopped briefly in Washington, D.C., to visit his brother Dwight, then in medical school. "Paul was really bubbling over with enthusiasm for the trip," Dwight recalls. "It was an inspiration to see him so happy and full of purpose."

Until he reached Leopoldville, Paul didn't know what section of Congo he would be assigned to, beyond the fact that it would certainly be to an understaffed hospital. The Congo Protestant Relief Agency's Operation Doctor program was not related to denominational mission groups in any way, but whenever possible, doctors were assigned to the areas served by their own denominations. When the agency's representatives in Leopoldville found that Paul belonged to the Covenant Church, they assigned him to Ubangi Province, where the Covenant Church worked, because there was a need for a doctor in that area.

A word of explanation should be given here regarding Christian mission work in Congo. Roman Catholic missions existed throughout Congo, having been established during the years of predominantly Catholic Belgium's rule. Protestant missions also spread throughout Congo, but each denomination worked within the area assigned to it originally by the Belgian government. The Evangelical Free Church of America entered Congo for mission work in the late 1920s, and was assigned to the northwestern part of Congo, the Ubangi region. In 1936 the Evangelical Covenant Church of America joined the Free Church in the Ubangi, and the two groups combined forces under the Free Church Charter, Mission Évangélique de l'Ubangi (MEU). Each mission had its own organization and personnel, but both groups worked in close harmony, holding frequent conferences and get-togethers to discuss questions and for fellowship. A dozen or more mission stations were established, the exact number varying over the years.

There were major tribal languages used in the Ubangi, in addition to the official language (French) and the trade language (Lingala). In mission work in the Ubangi, as I would soon learn for myself, the Congolese pastor had a key role. The pastor knew the tribal language, and his was the task of preaching and evangelizing. Primary schools were taught by Congolese. Congolese were trained as nurses. The missionary's role was that of adviser, and of teacher in secondary education, pastoral training, and medical training. The aim, of course, has to enable the Congolese to eventually staff and run all of their institutions.

Paul well knew when he went to Congo that he was going as one who serve the Congolese, which meant the church of whatever region he was assigned to, and that, in turn, meant stripping himself of certain privileges of authority as a trained medical man before the Congolese leadership. As Arden Almquist, executive secretary world missions (and himself a medical doctor who served in the Ubangi), explained: "Within months of national independence [June 30, 1960] the Ubangi Church found itself administering a large school system with Congolese replacing missionaries as directors, and several hospitals and dispensaries with Congolese instead of missionaries carrying responsibility as administrators."

With independence, most of the Belgian doctors in Congo fled. That meant that more than 700 of them departed. The resulting vacuum was such that many of the government hospitals had no doctors at all and many patients died from lack of care.

By the time Paul arrived, most of the doctors left in Congo were with the World Health Organization or were Protestant missionaries. En route to his assignment in the Ubangi, Paul stopped at the government medical school at Lovanium, in Leopoldville, where he got a hint of just what independence had meant to the teaching of medicine in Congo. At the school was another American volunteer, and he was the only chest surgeon in the entire Congo. Even though facilities in this medical school were superior by Congo standards, there was, for instance, no running hot water. The school had just recently graduated its first M.D.'s—three men.

"Medicine will never be established on a truly indigenous basis," Paul wrote to me, "until there are adequate doctors to staff the hospitals. As I see it, this achievement is still a long way off. In the meantime, Christian doctors have the unique opportunity of presenting Christ as they serve the people through medicine." Thus did Paul see his four-month term opening before him, and that was the attitude he carried with him in all his dealings with the Congolese.

In the Ubangi field, Paul met many people. Naomi Skoglund from Kingsburg, California, who had gone to the mission field the year that Paul was born, was assigned to him as nurse and interpreter. Naomi recalled that she had misgivings about working with a young, unknown doctor fresh from the United States. She feared that coming from the ease of fully equipped American hospitals, he might have a difficult time adjusting to the inadequacies of Congo medical facilities. But when they met, they found that they knew many of the same people in America, and they became an effective team with a great deal of mutual respect. Paul's first assignment was at the Tandala hospital, which had 120 beds, to help Dr. Carol Swartz, also out under Operation Doctor. She had not had training in surgery, and she wanted to learn some of the basic procedures. Paul helped her acquire the skills she needed there. Meanwhile, Paul got his first taste of operating in hospitals with equipment far different from what he was used to.

"At Libenge [Paul wrote of his experience in the government hospital there], we had no blood-pressure pump that worked, so we operated by 'pulse and prayer' most of the time."

"The disabled light plant meant that night operations were performed in kerosene lantern light."

"Being at a state hospital, the African nurses, who were always men, were unreliable. Drink was a major problem. We were constantly aware of the differences Christianity had made in the lives of the nurses at our mission hospital."

I knew from Paul's letters that he was very happy in his work and interested in his surroundings (as was the Paul I had always known). The typical government hospital, as Paul learned, during the time of Belgian rule was staffed by Belgian doctors with Catholic sisters as nurses. Male Congolese acted as nurses and assistants around the hospital. After independence, in the absence of the Belgian doctors in Congo, medical standards deteriorated markedly within a few months. Among the medical missionaries carrying on were Warren and Gretchen Berggren, assigned at that time to a government hospital. Both of them were suffering severe fatigue as a result of the heavy load of work occasioned by the departure of the Belgian doctors.

"We were exhausted," Dr. Gretchen wrote of this time. "We prayed that somehow we would be able to finish the time we had promised to serve. One day a young surgeon from California arrived in response to our S-O-S. He greeted us with a warm smile, eagerly made rounds in a 200-bed hospital with us. In a few days he was performing surgery with a very limited number of instruments under conditions that Americans consider primitive. The Congolese liked him immediately. He didn't complain about the lack of facilities; there was a need. He came to fill it, and to send us on our needed vacation. . . . The cheerful optimism with which he sent us on our way buoyed us up."

After the Berggrens' vacation, Paul was a "guest surgeon" for a day at Bosobolo, a government hospital. Here, where he was the first American doctor to operate in that hospital, he was keenly aware of how standards had lowered. "If a nurse needed an instrument for a second case," Paul wrote to me, "he thought nothing of taking one that had been used for the first. He didn't bother to change gloves between spinals, either. By the time he came to the third case, he merely rinsed the blood from the instrument before handing it to me. I cringed, but what could I do? I was there only as a *guest*—the Congolese were in charge. I'd just bite my lips, and with as much grace as I could muster, use the sutures that were given me (some were as heavy as rope, it seemed) and trust God to cover 'a multitude of sins.'"

Finally, Paul was assigned to Wasolo in the northeasternmost corner of the field, and a long time away from everywhere. With Paul and Naomi at Wasolo was Jody LeVahn, who was assigned to the station. Because mission board policy forbids a woman to stay alone on a station, Jody was working at Karawa during that period. At the time Paul was there, she had just returned from furlough. Paul's stay at Wasolo was his longest stay at any hospital during his short term. His letters home revealed how much he was learning, how enjoyable he found the work, and a growing desire to return on a permanent basis. The overwhelming medical needs of the Congolese touched him, and the strangeness of the surroundings intrigued him.

The spiritual high spot of Paul's short term was the "Big Sunday" meeting at a Norwegian Baptist station at the village of Dongbe, across the Uele River from Wasolo.

"The Africans [at Dongbe] had been without missionary direction for some time," Paul wrote. "Because floods had made some of the roads impassable, we waded through mud and mire and rode dugout canoes to get there." Naomi and Jody had also been invited, and the three of them crossed the Uele in a pirogue. As the rowers maneuvered the canoe, they chanted in rhythm with the paddle strokes:

"Oyo mondeli monganga akumi... kopesa biso malamu mingi... Ye kopesa... biso maloba na Nzambe... pelamoko kopesa biso mono mpo na njoto malamu...." ("This is the white doctor who has come to give us much good.... He will give... us words of God... just as he will give us medicine for a well body....") This was their description of the *monganga* and his two helpers coming up river to carry the story of Jesus Christ to another village.

As they came ashore, they were greeted by the beating of drums and a large crowd of villagers. The drums also summoned people from the surrounding jungle to the Big Sunday services.

Paul, Naomi, and Jody, as guests of honor, were ushered into the chapel, with its red mud walls and thatched roof, and onto the platform. Some 200 villagers had assembled and sat expectantly, the men many in loincloths and vests and the women with their wrap-around garments, awaiting the testimonies of their guests. Paul spoke in English on the text John 14:6, "I am the way; I am the truth and I am life; no one comes to the Father except by me," after which Jody translated his words into Lingala. Then an African pastor translated the Lingala into the tribal language. Altogether during that meeting, five languages (two trade languages, the tribal language, French, and English) were used.

Big Sunday was more than just a Sunday—it was a whole weekend of services. A highlight of the weekend was the baptism of new Christians. The ceremony was performed in the river and the candidates for baptism approached dressed in hospital gowns, so that they were all in white. One by one, they were taken down into the river and the service of baptism was conducted by the African pastor. Paul, with the others, watched from the shore. He was greatly impressed by the obvious change in commitment in the lives of these people who had accepted Christ. Happiness shone from their faces as they emerged from the waters. Around them were their relatives who had taken this step at an earlier date now rejoicing in the sight of their brothers and sisters taking the same step. It was a day of great joy.

The villagers showed their appreciation for the visit of the missionaries by giving them such foods as a chicken, eggs, oranges, bananas, and pineapples.

After his time at Wasolo station was up, Paul decided to go back to Tandala by way of Goyongo, where there was a pastors' training school and a Bible institute. At this particular time, the annual conference of the Congolese Church* was in progress. Naomi, who was still with Paul as interpreter, recalled being approached by Joseph Doko, then president of the Ubangi Church, with the words, "I want you to tell Dr. Paul Carlson that we want him to come back to Congo as our missionary doctor."

Paul's response was one of great joy and humility. He was thrilled that he had won a place with these people, and he told Pastor Doko how pleased and thankful he was for the invitation and that he would make it a matter of prayer. There were, of course, many considerations: his family's reactions, whether the mission board of the Covenant Church would send the family out, whether financing was available.

Normally, a mission board decides to send someone out, and then asks a particular candidate if he or she will go. To be invited by the national church first is unusual. It was with added happiness and lightheartedness that Paul returned to the Tandala station, where he had started his work nearly four months earlier, having Pastor Doko's assurance that the Ubangi Church would send a formal request to the mission board in the United States to have him and his family sent out.

Paul would be going home soon; yet work remained to be done. A Congolese Bible teacher at Tandala named Joseph Penzi had been troubled with ulcers for a long time. Paul had seen him previously and now saw him again. He felt that only surgery could help Penzi. The equipment and set-up was such that surgery to do a gastrectomy, which is partial removal of the stomach, was a

---

*At that time the church organization in the Ubangi was referred to as the ECU for the French *Église du Christ de l'Ubangi*, which translates "Church of Christ of the Ubangi." However, the usual English title is "Evangelical Church of the Ubangi."

dangerous operation there. Paul decided that he would try, however, if he could locate some necessary equipment. A plea was made over the radio network:

This is Nine-Q-Three-Four to all stations... Does anyone have a tank of oxygen? Dr. Paul must have oxygen for Penzi's surgery as soon as possible.... Over.

It was nearing Paul's departure date from Congo, and oxygen would have to be secured quickly. They waited for a reply. At last the transmitter at another station clicked on, and the loudspeaker in the radio room at Tandala began to vibrate:

Nine-Q-Three-Four, this is Nine-Q-Three-Seven calling.... This is Nine-Q-Three-Seven to Nine-Q-Three-Four. There's some oxygen in a tank here that Harv used for welding. We can bring that with us as far as Gemena tomorrow.... Over.

This was Bokada station. Harvey Widman, a missionary evangelist, occasionally did some welding repairs but was on furlough at the time. Consequently the oxygen supply required for his work was not being used.

Three-Four to Three-Seven. Roger. Thank you. We will send a truck to Gemena tomorrow to pick it up.

By the time the oxygen arrived, other preparations for Penzi's important and difficult surgery were complete. Everyone prayed that the operation would go well.

Fortunately the light plant worked properly, providing adequate light and power for the suction machine, which was necessary for the surgery. The anesthesia available, however, left much to be desired. The oxygen supply helped to maintain Penzi's regular breathing while the operation was in progress. Paul improvised many things. He was not easily discouraged. He did not have another trained surgeon to assist as he would have had in America. In fact, no other doctor was available. Dr. Carol Swartz, although still at Tandala, was very ill at the time. Naomi and other missionary nurses at the station were his assistants.

Tenseness filled the air as Penzi's family, his students, the station pastor, villagers, and missionaries awaited the outcome of surgery of a type that had not previously been performed with so few supplies.

The operation was a success. The missionary nurses took turns watching and caring for Penzi for several days. This was a new concept in nursing for the Congolese nurses. Usually, a relative of the patient would accompany him to the hospital and cares for him afterward. However well-meaning such care, it was hardly adequate in many cases. The Congolese watched and marveled at the expert and tender care given this man whom they all loved. They were highly impressed with Paul's surgery, particularly when Penzi recovered rapidly, and was restored to health as a result of it.

In the course of his four-month tour, Paul formed firmer and firmer beliefs about the need for expanded training for personnel in medical work—bedside nursing for the comfort of patients, careful watching of postoperative cases, and other kinds of medical care that are conventional nursing in the United States. The frustration to Paul was that, although he often could perform large operations with makeshift equipment, the lack of proper aftercare might completely undo his work and prevent the recovery of the patients on whom he had worked so hard. Postoperative nursing care and training became a burden and a concern of his, which he carried with him from that time on.

The success of Penzi's surgery spread like a drum message to all stations in the Ubangi and it served further to establish Paul in the esteem of the Congolese, which again made him happy and content with his short term in Congo. The people realized that the kind of surgery Penzi had was of a sort not often performed on a remote mission station, but that with better training and supplies, it could be done.

I V

So Send I You

Christmas 1961 was a happy one for the Carlsons. Paul returned early in December, and for the first time in five years he was free of the usual commitments of a busy doctor. It seemed almost unbelievable that we could accept invitations from friends and relatives for parties, take in choir concerts at Christmastime, and join in family festivities without having to fit them into a crowded, on-call schedule at the hospital.

Wayne and Lyn virtually bubbled over with joy and enthusiasm at having their daddy home again.

As the days passed I became increasingly aware that the Paul Carlson who had returned from Congo was a new person—no, not a different person, but the Paul Carlson I had known in earlier years. His attitudes had changed, his ideals shone forth again, his purposes in life were well defined, his outlook on the future was confident. I knew that Paul had come back to himself and back to his God. What the future held for us, whether the way to service in Congo would open for us, we didn't know, but we felt that the direction was becoming evident.

Meanwhile, interlaced among the festivities of the Christmas holidays, with the smörgåsbord traditional in our family, was the reality we had to face. We had a house. We had responsibilities. We had to come to some kind of a decision about medical practice in America. Our finances were at a low ebb. At this point, the group of doctors with whom Paul had worked part time while in residency made him an offer to come into practice with them as their second surgeon. We were very happy with the thoughtfulness of these men and for their confidence in Paul professionally. Paul had enjoyed working with them during his years of training, and had a high regard for their methods of practice. This also made us happy as a family because it meant that we would not have to move elsewhere. Things could go on in relatively normal fashion and there would not be any great uprooting at this time of indecision when we still didn't know whether we would finally be going to Congo or not.

Paul was always honest with people so, pleased and grateful as he was with this offer, he told the doctors of his strong feeling about further missionary work, and of the request made by the Ubangi Evangelical Church. Their reply was that they wanted him anyway, and if later he felt he should return to Congo, they would understand. Thus, on the first of January 1962, Paul went into practice with the Redondo Beach Medical Clinic.

At this same time, Paul was elected chair of our local church, Rolling Hills Covenant Church, which we had joined at its organization in the late 1950s. He plunged into his new role with a zeal that I had not seen in him since North Park days, when I first met him. His energy had been dulled through the long years of intensive study, preparation, and work. Now, however, when he came back mentally and spiritually refreshed from Congo, he had a great renewal of zeal for the work of the church and for its potential. He felt his enthusiasm ought to be applied liberally to church work. It was an inspiration for me to watch him, and I more than once marveled at his tirelessness on behalf of the church.

As chair, he was the chief lay officer of the congregation, and one of his most important duties was acting as chair of the church board when it met, which often meant harmonizing conflicting views of board members. Paul had a facility for keeping organizations within the church running smoothly, and for preventing natural differences of view from going beyond healthy debate into acrimony or divisive argument. Also, in the absence of a pastor, the chair would lead the services although he would not preach or perform the sacraments.

Paul was happy in practice and very interested in each of his patients. I often marveled at his patience in telephone conversations at odd hours and his ability to become fully awakened at night and usually have the phone off the hook before it stopped the first ring—and be pleasant in answering. He was very cautious in surgery diagnosis. More than once I recall him tossing and turning in bed at night, pondering whether to operate or not, and I'd say, "Please go and operate so you can come home and get some sleep."

Both of us were happy in what we were doing, in the way the days seemed to organize themselves into interesting patterns, in the growth and development of our two children, in the fact that our good friends and relatives again played an important part in our less crowded schedule. We led a rather busy social life at this time.

It was, of course, a comfortable feeling to know that we had a better income. Now we could purchase some of the things that we had not been able to afford during the years of training. It was becoming a pleasant kind of life that one could easily get used to and not want to abandon.

Then came March 1962. In the mail one day was a letter from the executive secretary of world missions of the Evangelical Covenant Church of America in Chicago. Paul ripped the envelope open and we read it together. The words leaped out at us: "We would like to send your family to Congo if funds become available and if you are still willing."

I could see the radiance and joy in Paul's face. I could not say anything. I walked to the other end of the room because I did not want him to see the tears. He came over to me then and he didn't have to ask what was wrong. He was sensitive to the feelings of others, and he knew the struggle that was going on within his wife.

Putting his arm around me he said, "Honey, we both must want to go, or else it will not be good."

I knew what my answer would be, but I couldn't voice it then. In a sense I had given him the answer about twelve years before. My mind flashed to the difficult years so recently behind us, and I knew definitely that my prayers for Paul at the time of his confusion had been answered. Now I found that I was the one in a state of confusion. Why? Why was my heart rebelling now? Why, when I knew that this was the work we both were being called to?

It was so easy to look to the undemanding side of life, to look forward to a comfortable existence. It was easy to look forward with our medical colleagues to a better standard of living, as we Americans term it, in that we have all the comforts money can buy. We were on the verge of attaining that kind of life, and now we were faced with the decision that had to be made, that we had known would have to be made—and it had to be made by both of us.

We talked about it. We prayed about it. We talked over the effects the children might suffer by going into a foreign country. We reviewed the problems of schooling. On that point, because Paul had been in Congo and had seen the school situation firsthand, he was confident: "I can see no reason from the schooling standpoint why that should be a factor in our not going," he said. The school set-up, he pointed out, was excellent.

Then the question, "Is it right for a family to be separated?" arose. We knew that were we to go the children would be away from us for about two months at a time, and for nine months out of the year, living in a mission school dormitory. We sought out other missionaries who had been in Congo and asked them about this problem. We talked to their children about the schools: what courses they took, how they liked it, whether their separation from home seemed to be a serious problem. We could see no ill effects at all. They were happy, well-adjusted children who uniformly said they wanted to go back to Congo, and that being away from home was an agreeable adventure, not an occasion for sadness.

Some of my questions and excuses for not going were evaporating before my eyes. We talked still more and we prayed more than ever. Neither of us had any doubt in our minds what our answer should be. As Paul so often said in his talks to various groups, "One can't come back from an African visit like mine without feeling one's Christian responsibility tremendously. In Africa I knew I was doing something that wouldn't get done if I weren't there. Here I know there are plenty of others who can do the job I am doing." Yes, we must go. It was our Christian responsibility to go to these people. The Congolese had asked us to come. I knew in my heart what the answer must be. After the long discussions, the reflection, the consideration, and the prayer, we sent a letter to the secretary of the mission board saying, "Yes, we are willing to be sent when you can send us."

Just at this time, as Paul's practice was increasing, the work in our local church was growing heavier. Our pastor had left to take a pastorate at another church, and the Rolling Hills church was to be without a minister for three months. This put an extra burden on Paul, as chair, because he had to take on responsibilities of leadership that ordinarily fall to the pastor. Not unnaturally there was a letdown in effort on the part of the church members. "Let's not do anything now; let's wait until our new pastor comes," was the prevailing attitude. Paul was deeply concerned over the trend and one night, after coming home from a church board meeting, he exclaimed, "Something has to be done at the church!" He sat down at his typewriter and for nearly an hour typed steadily. Finally, pausing in my mending, I interrupted him long enough to ask, "Honey, what are you doing?"

"I'm making out a program called 'One Hundred Days of Preparation' for the church."

I put down my sewing and walked over to look at the proposed plan. "This is rather ambitious, isn't it? You're lining up a whole program. Do you think the people will follow through on it?"

"I don't know. But we have to start somewhere. When I finish writing this out, I'll see what the board thinks about it, and whether they have suggestions—I'm sure they will—and just see what kind of a program we can line up. If we can keep our members on their toes during this waiting time, we'll have a better and more dedicated congregation."

Paul resumed his typing, and it was 2 a.m. before he stopped. The church board did accept it, with minor changes.

Paul well knew that the summer months are often a lag period in church work, and he and the board members felt that if they were to succeed, it would be through rescuing this summer "waste time" and making it productive time. Since this summer doldrum period was also an interim period between pastors in our church, the temptation to "let down" was even greater.

The "kickoff dinner" opening the One Hundred Days of Preparation was a great success, and everyone was excited about the forthcoming program. The whole period became a time of growth and zealous activity in our church. One of the additional tasks Paul set himself was to write a weekly letter to the incoming pastor in which he sought to set forth the main problems that the new pastor would have to face, and the opportunities, as Paul saw them, that were open for both minister and congregation. As it was a fast-growing area and as the congregation had every prospect of corresponding growth, the opportunities, Paul believed, were great.

Toward the end of May, shortly after the launching of this campaign, we received word from the executive secretary of world missions that funds had been appropriated for our assignment to Congo. By this time, of course, our decision was firm, and we were happy now to be able to make definite plans. In June 1962 we attended the Covenant Annual Meeting in Seattle. After the banquet on the last night of the conference, attended by some 2,000 people, the new missionaries were commissioned. Paul and I, along with others, offered our testimony and joined in the great missionary hymn, "So Send I You," as we dedicated ourselves to follow Christ's admonition to his disciples, "Go forth therefore and make all nations my disciples."

From that service we flew back to our home in Torrance and set about the business of buying and packing, which seemed to be endless. We had to get clothing for the children and ourselves for a three-year term. Just the challenge of buying shoes—trying to guess how much in sizes the children would grow in a three-year period—seemed to me a big obstacle to overcome. Then everything went into fifty-five gallon drums for shipping overseas. During the time of packing, many dear friends wanted to have us to dinner, for parties, and for get togethers. So we had a busy summer full of fun and excitement and good fellowship as we prepared to leave.

We were also becoming acquainted with the news media. Newspaper reporters began to call, asking why this doctor who had started in practice in the area wanted to become a missionary doctor. Paul's response to them was the same one he had given so many times to groups where he had been asked to show slides and tell of his work during those four months in Congo: "Here there are so many to do the work—over there so few."

We finally completed arrangements to rent our home during our time in Congo. We had decided to keep the house as we felt this would provide a permanent base so that we could come back to familiar territory and to surroundings we loved during our furlough time, which would be in a little over three years. Beyond that, we wanted to provide stability for the children, as much as we could, and we knew that they could remember their home, remember their church, and would want to come back during the time we would have between terms on the mission field.

So it was that at the end of August the last lid went on the last fifty-five-gallon drum, the last cupboard was cleaned, the last floor was polished, ready for the renters who would soon be moving in. We, meanwhile, finished our preparations for a cross-country trip to visit my family in Michigan, where the children and I were to stay while Paul took a three-month course in tropical medicine at Liverpool, England.

From England, where he was living with an English family in Rock Ferry, near Liverpool, Paul wrote: "The course is heavy. It's like being at medical school again, but not quite as long hours. We begin at ten o'clock in the morning with a lecture, and then possibly another at eleven, or perhaps a laboratory. The lecturing resumes at noon. Then, at two, another lecture followed by a second, or perhaps a lab. We are running four subjects, so it is no snap. About forty-five doctors from all over the world (except for Russia and South America) are studying here. They come from India, Egypt, Africa."

In mid-December, the children and I flew to England. After a brief vacation for Paul, and sightseeing for all of us, we went to Paris just before Christmas, where we were to study French (the official language in Congo) for six months.

We studied French diligently—Paul taking a five-hour-a-day course and I a two-hour-a-day one. I was having to learn, also, how to shop in Paris. Having to go to a different store for each grocery item was a new experience for me. Many weeks passed before I realized that one bought yeast in a bakery, not in a grocery store.

Wayne and Lyn were enrolled in a French school. At first they shy about this strange land, but they adjusted quickly and soon were beginning to correct our French pronunciation. Lyn mastered the French "r" more readily than the rest of us.

Our studies ended in June, and on July 6 we were on our way again. On the flight from Paris to Africa, Paul wanted to make several stops in order to check on leads he had received concerning the purchase of medicines and surgical instruments. Also, he believed in seeing as much as he could when the opportunity presented itself, in case he should not chance that way again. So we had a delightful stop in Zurich, and decided that this was a place we would like someday to spend a vacation. We made stops in Florence, Milan, Pisa, Venice, and Rome. With our departure from Rome, we left Europe and headed for Africa—on the last lap of our journey to our future work.

V

Arrival in Africa

Our immediate destination was Bangui, Central African Republic, the closest airfield to our Congo objective that could accommodate large planes. As we came in for the landing, Paul pointed out the Ubangi River, winding through the deep greens of the jungle, and showed us how Congo and the Central African Republic sit side by side, divided by the Ubangi.

Then the tires were squealing on the runway and the plane lurched a bit, and we were taxiing to the arrivals building. We knew we were in Africa when the doors opened and the humid air engulfed us like a hot blanket.

We had stopped at so many airports in the last twelve days with no one to greet us that it was a thrill to see Paul's cousins, Frank and Margaret Lindquist, who were missionaries in the Ubangi, and Dr. Teddy Johnson, another Covenant missionary, whom we had met before when she was on furlough, waving their greetings as we stepped off the plane. We felt a certain sense of incongruity when we realized how many thousands of miles we were from home, yet in this strange land we were being greeted by relatives. Frank and Margaret were to take us to Karawa, where we would study Lingala for three months before going on to our permanent post, Wasolo station.

We spent about a day and a half in Bangui, where there were dental appointments for the Lindquists and shopping for items that could not be bought in the Republic of Congo. "This is your last look at civilization for a while," we were kiddingly told. Bangui was very French in character, with a large number of expatriates, especially Europeans, and with embassies from most of the major powers, including the United States and China. Even though it was a city without paved streets, it had stores with many products for sale, most of them French-made, hotels, restaurants, cars, and other things to remind one of a small city anywhere. But other things proclaimed it as African. The water fountain in the square sent its cooling spray upward in the midst of a stand of palms. The colorful outdoor market was the most popular meeting place for Africans, for whom it was a social occasion as well as a place for selling their fruits and vegetables. In addition, many Arab traders were around, selling everything from ivory figurines to clothing and yard goods.

After two days of errands in Bangui, we left the city behind. This time our travel was by pirogue and truck. As we carried our luggage down the Ubangi River embankment, I had my first sight of a pirogue, which is actually an entire tree trunk that has been hollowed out and shaped to move swiftly through the water. We happened to take one rigged with an outboard motor, so we crossed quickly, but still it was a bit frightening because the dugout canoe sits so low in the water. I had the uneasy feeling that the slightest wavelet or rocking of the boat would be enough to send it to the bottom. The Ubangi River at this point has many whirlpools that must be dodged.

We landed on a sandy strip of shore, and were in Zongo, Ubangi Province, Republic of Congo, which meant that we had to go through customs before we could continue. We held our breath, hoping that things would not become difficult. One day, the officials would make you display everything and would charge a lot. The next day they would merely glance in one trunk and might charge very little. They were lenient with us and let us by without much opening, unpacking, or charge.

Frank and Margaret had the mission truck for us, and we piled our belongings into the back of it; then the four Lindquist children and our two, Dr. Teddy, and Paul hopped in alongside them. I rode in the cab with Frank and Margaret. We were off on a jostling, jouncing ride on a rutted, one-lane dirt road. How the mission trucks lasted even as long as they did was a miracle. The children thought it a grand adventure as they rode in the back of the truck. Many of the bridges we crossed made us hold our breath and whisper a prayer, they were so flimsy looking. As we drove along at the breakneck speed of twenty miles per hour, we always had to be on guard for the ever-present chickens, pigs, and goats, which had to cross just as a car approached. The children claimed that our mortality that day amounted to three chickens and a goat, but we seriously doubted the goat.

Our first stop was to be Bokada, Dr. Teddy's station. With luck, we would make it in three hours. Even so, it would be dark by the time we arrived.

Grassland surrounded us. The rolling, grassy mounds we passed were actually old anthills overgrown with vegetation, and the steeple-shaped grayish-brown mounds were new anthills. Looking across an expanse of land, we could see scores of these hills. The sobi grass, as it is called, was greenish brown and rustled in the wind. It grows shoulder high, or even as high as the cab of the truck in some places, and is typical of the grassland plateau of the Ubangi region. However, the Ubangi topography varies greatly from place to place, and as I was soon to see with my own eyes, the grassland of the Bokada area gives way to deep jungle growth around Goyongo.

Now and again we would pass a small village, some having no more than six houses, others containing scores of mud huts, round in shape with sobi-grass thatch for roofs. When the village children heard the truck coming in the distance, they would run to the side of the road and stand in groups, waving to us as we came along. Occasionally a man would run out with his little baby and hold it up so we could see it as we passed. They were proud of their children and this was a way of saying, "Here is my baby. I want you to see him." As dusk gathered and the people were preparing their evening meals, a pall of smoke hung near the villages because their fires were going full force. We could see the families gathered around their little fires with a stewpot in the center of the flames. They sat on the ground, or sometimes on their low bamboo beds, which they had pulled up close to the fire. Trucks did not pass by often, and the Congolese always gave us a cheerful wave.

Suddenly a small bridge appeared before us. To me it looked like a few sticks laid across the gully, and I was not far wrong as it turned out, because the logs had not been lashed together. Frank slowed the truck and then stopped it altogether.

"I don't think we should all stay in the truck," Paul said, after surveying the situation.

"You mean we might fall in?" I asked, looking down at the small stream.

"Yes," Frank said.

So we all piled out, and Margaret, Dr. Teddy, and I, taking the children, walked gingerly over the bridge. Paul stayed on the other side to help Frank guide the truck across. After we crossed the logs—about seventeen feet in length—we watched the men as they began very slowly to move the truck onto the bridge. (Actually the only thing I could see at that moment was all our belongings at the bottom of the stream with us hours from any place where we could possibly get help.) As the wheels touched the logs and the truck started across, the branches of the roadbed began jumping up just like pick-up sticks, popping up at every angle and then falling down and settling into place again.

When we finally arrived at Bokada station, dusty and hot, we were met by Dr. Teddy's cook, who had a hot meal and, perhaps what we appreciated even more, warm bucket showers ready for us. It took a long time to cover a short distance in Congo, and the warmest hospitality a host could show a traveler was to offer a shower and a good meal after a dusty day on the road, during which the principal food had been too-warm sandwiches.

A bucket shower was an experience I will never forget. We would come off the truck, orange with dust, looking like something from outer space. The shower, which might be on a porch enclosed by a grass-mat screen, consisted of a small overhead pail, with a sprinkler head and valve arrangement that permits water to dribble down. A few moments under one of those almost wiped from memory the six or eight hours of jouncing along a rutted road.

After a night of resting, we were again on our way to Karawa. We reached Goyongo station, where the Evangelical Church of the Ubangi (ECU) Bible school and seminary were located, in time for lunch. The Lundquist and

Monson families lived at this station and taught school for the Congolese students there. I was particularly happy to see Goyongo, because it was here that Pastor Joseph Doko, then president of the ECU, had made his official invitation to Paul to return to Congo. We had to hurry on immediately after lunch because we wanted to be at Karawa that night.

Karawa is built on a hill, and as we approached it that evening, we could see the lights in the distance. At the entrance to the station a big "MBOTE" sign (the traditional Lingala greeting) hung across the road. The African pastor had strung it there for us. As we drove up, tooting our horn to announce our arrival, the missionaries came bursting out of the buildings to greet us and to install us in the house that was to be our home for the next three months.

When we awakened the next morning, we began to appreciate how lovely a place Karawa is. Palm trees and tropical foliage of a luscious green surrounded us. The temperature was not uncomfortable, and at night it turned fairly cool, so we had no trouble sleeping. Tropical rains came often to refresh us, but they played havoc with the dirt roads. As I wrote my parents shortly afterward: "This could well be a tropical paradise, but there is much work to be done, so one can't just loaf."

Our Karawa home was an adobe house, whitewashed, and with a sobi-grass roof that made it picturesque but also created unexpected problems—such as insects falling on us from the roof while we were eating or sleeping. This was the only house at Karawa station without hardboard ceilings. The thatch roof was an efficient shield against the heat of the day, however, as were the white walls. The house was very cool. The windows were screened, without glass but equipped with shutters on the outside of the house that could be closed whenever it rained or turned cold. Occasionally in the middle of the night the wind would commence rustling through the sobi-grass thatch and through the trees outside. We knew that meant a storm was on the way, so we would hurry out to close the shutters.

At Karawa we found that Dr. Helen Berquist, whom we had known during North Park College days, and who was to return from furlough a week after we arrived, had been delayed, so Paul had to divide his time between medicine and Lingala studies. The children were very happy at Karawa, as there were several boys for Wayne to play with and two little girls about Lyn's age. They roamed the station, prowled under every tree, and explored who knows what else. On our third day there, one of our friends gave the children a baby monkey, but we had a funeral within a week, and none of us wanted another pet monkey for a while—we had become so attached to that one.

At first I didn't know how I would manage with a cook, a Congolese man hired to do the cooking and the bulk of the housework, but within a few weeks I didn't know how I could get along without someone to cook on a wood stove, to boil and filter water, to iron with a charcoal iron, to bake the bread, to bargain with the women who came to sell things, and to do many other of the endless chores.

Paul wrote to his brother: "The tom-toms have gone out. There is a doctor here at Karawa again, so the patients are beginning to trickle in. Most of them are real headache cases, but not many psychosomatic. We are thankful to be here, enjoying the fellowship, waiting to go on to Wasolo, where we will be. Our food has arrived in Bangui, so we will make the trek up there next week for it. Our barrels were due to be here on the 25th of June. They have not yet come, but we have no great needs, and everyone lends a bit here and a bit there. The shipment of drugs is here, so we feel we are getting on our feet. There is much to do. There has not been a regular doctor at Wasolo on a permanent basis for about three years now, so there will be rearranging and so forth, but this offers challenges."

The first thing at Karawa, was, of course, language study, and for a while it seemed to me that the principal result of my six-month French course, just past, was to confuse me in Lingala. Knowing that the Congolese around me did not understand English, my automatic reaction was to reach for the first foreign word I could think of. It always came out French. With concentration and hard work, I began to acquire a Lingala vocabulary. Paul had similar difficulty, but he seemed to make faster progress than I. We learned not only in our Lingala class, taught by a missionary with a Congolese assistant, but also from the Congolese themselves with whom we came in contact each day. Someone would point to an object and say the word for it. We would repeat the word, and if we pronounced it incorrectly, we would repeat it again and again until we got it right. There are high tones and low tones, and it is important to learn the different meanings the tone gives to a word. For example, two words have the same spelling and pronunciation, but in one the final syllable is said with a rising tone, and in the other, the voice drops on the final syllable. One word means "peanut" and the other means "spear." So, you say the wrong word and you get the wrong thing. Another example concerns the words for "to know" and "to steal." They are very similar, and you can judge the importance of correctness there.

Paul and I drilled each other outside of classes, and we tried to speak only Lingala at the dinner table, but that didn't work because the children at this time were not in sufficient contact with the language. There were several missionary children at the station, so they continued to talk in English. We tried to converse more and more with Azupka, our cook, and he was very patient and understanding and of tremendous help. Our progress was further complicated by the fact that Paul and I needed different basic vocabularies. I had to be able to give directions to Azupka, to instruct the girl students I would have at Wasolo in such things as sewing, whereas Paul needed to be able to ask people where they hurt, what region they were from, and things like that. I remember saying more than once that it would be easier for me to go ahead and do the thing myself rather than explain to someone else how to do it. In addition, there were many tribal customs to learn about and local standards of courtesy to become sensitive to.

Besides problems of language and culture, I had lessons to learn about housekeeping. For example, any of the grain-type foods had to be kept in tins—that meant rice, macaroni, and spaghetti. Our flour also came in tins. When our order of food arrived, we had to borrow a lot of flour tins because I didn't have any empty ones. Many items would be put down in packing barrels—brown sugar and powdered sugar, for instance. I still remember the dried kidney beans and peas that I had put down in a barrel: several months later I opened it, and weevils flew out, as though it were Pandora's box.

In a letter written to our families, dated August 18, 1963, just a month after our arrival at Karawa, we described the method of getting meat: "Friday a couple of the missionary men butchered beef for the station. Each missionary family buys so much per person. A good part of yesterday was spent cutting, grinding hamburger, and packaging the meats. We have a fair-sized freezing compartment in the refrigerator, so it works out well. We certainly could use a big freezer out here. The only hitch would be that it would have to be run by kerosene as are the refrigerators. We are going to inquire about kerosene freezers. The dormitory could use one, especially. They have two refrigerators, but with thirty children living here, they go through a lot of food."

Karawa is the station where the Ubangi Academy, the school for the missionary children, is located, and soon Wayne would be living in that dormitory. About a month after our arrival, classes began for the children. One Monday all the families from the entire Ubangi field brought their children in to begin school, so it was a great time to get to know those from the field whom we did not know, to renew acquaintances with those we had known in America. The school had three rooms: one for the second through fourth grades, another for the fifth through seventh, and a third for the high school children. That year was the first time they had included a complete high school with a senior class in the academy. There were three full-time teachers, and Bob Peterson, the dormitory father, also taught part-time in the high school.

Bob and Ruth Ann Peterson were kept busy as dormitory parents, for, including their family, thirty-five were living there that year. The children enjoyed being together, and they have fond memories of the times at Ubangi Academy. Sessions ran about nine weeks at a time, with vacation between, so the children who were away from their parents were not gone for extended periods, as is so often the case on mission fields. We felt we were fortunate in the educational arrangements on the field. Wayne and Lynette started school while we were still at Karawa; with Paul and me studying too, we were indeed a school family.

A letter I wrote to my parents describes some of the events of this time: "Paul has been busy with hospital work this week. As the word gets out that there is a doctor here, people start coming in more. Art Zylstra [a Covenant missionary visiting from Chicago for a survey in radio work] got quite a thrill the other noon. We were waiting for Paul for dinner. He was doing a Caesarean section, and I thought that if all went well, he should be just about done, so

Art said he would walk down and see. He got there just as Paul was lifting out a baby boy. He had never seen a baby come out that way, so was just delighted. There is no privacy in the operating room here. One can look in at any time. In fact, it is a real problem keeping the African relatives out of the way so one can work. They are doing some remodeling in the operating room, and Paul is trying to figure out a little viewing room on the side, to hold only one person. They wish him luck—the nurses that is; guess the Africans just have to see what is going on."

At the same time, we had two other visitors from Chicago, Dr. Fernly Johnson and his son Ron. Dr. Fernly was a surgeon at Swedish Covenant Hospital in Chicago. We were delighted to have them as visitors. We knew what Dr. Fernly meant when he said that by the time he reached Karawa, he didn't care to travel over any more bumpy roads. The first Sunday afternoon they were visiting, Paul wanted to have the Congolese nurses from the hospital along with the missionary nurses in for coffee. Many of the Congolese nurses—all men, of course—brought their wives along to the party, and we had a good time that afternoon. Other than for the party, it had been a normal Sunday at the station. The church service was at 8:30 a.m., when the Congolese pastor preaches and the service is conducted in Lingala. For the children in the dormitory, two or three missionaries had Sunday-school classes in English. In the evening the missionaries gathered in the little chapel for a brief service in English. A portable pump organ provided music.

After six months of French sermons and hymns in Paris, it was a thrill to attend a service in English again. After a few days of rest from the bumpy roads (no rest from hospital work), Dr. Fernly was persuaded by Paul to make a visit to Wasolo. I was eager to have my first glimpse of the place that would soon be our home. "They'll be so disappointed back home if you don't get to see some of the other stations," Paul said. So he, Ron, and Art Zylstra, who was still with us, decided to make the long trip to Wasolo—it usually took two days from Karawa because the roads were so poor.

Jody LeVahn, who was now working at Karawa until we moved to Wasolo, went along with us, as did Elsie Carlson (another missionary nurse, but not related to us), Lyn, and Azupka. We spent the first night at Gbado, the station where Frank and Margaret Lindquist were, and of course we enjoyed that evening.

We started out early the next morning, Saturday, because it was still a full day's trip to Wasolo. I had been warned that this was at the end of nowhere, out in the sticks, way up at the end of the world. I thought we would never get there—it seemed to be an endless road. On trips like that one, when you gaze up at the jungle and the high trees, and see an occasional monkey scurry across a branch or catch a glimpse of a bright-winged bird, you wonder how you could manage on foot, and I presume you couldn't. I remember hearing stories of the occasional tree that would fall across the road between Gbado and Wasolo, and the trouble that would ensue. How, for example, one time Dr. Arden Almquist, when he was the doctor at Wasolo, had faced that problem on this very road, and how he had enlisted the help of a group of villagers living nearby to chop through a huge old tree. It had taken them hours and hours, but they had succeeded, and at last the truck could resume its journey.

That day there was no fallen tree, no washed-out bridge, no other obstruction. But even so, the road seemed endless, and I began to doubt that we would ever get there. Then Paul told me to watch ahead, and we turned into the road that he said was from Targini, about seven kilometers (five miles) from the station.

"Is this the road!" I exclaimed.

Paul laughed, assuring me that it was. He explained that it was used principally as a bicycle lane, for few trucks passed that way. Then we crossed another rickety bridge, but by this time I did not go through the agonies of doubt that I had with the bridge on the way to Bokada. On the far side of the bridge was grass, grown so high that it reached above the roof of the truck. "My goodness," I thought, "they told me this place was way out nowhere, but I'm just not prepared for this."

Then suddenly, at a fork in the road, a little clearing broke, and there, lo and behold, was the sign reading "WASOLO." Immediately ahead I saw the cream-colored hospital. It was new, having been built just before Congo independence in 1960. In front of the hospital, a crowd of people waited, smiling and waving and saying "*Mbote*," and then stretching out their hands for us to shake. We could hardly get out of the truck, there were so many people. They hadn't seen a missionary truck, especially one with eight missionaries in it, for some time, and they were glad to see us.

Finally we finished our *Mbote's* and the handshaking. Dusk was falling and we wanted to go up Wasolo hill to Jody's home. Close by was the house we would be living in. Although Jody was not living at Wasolo then, she did get up occasionally to see that things were all right.

One of the first jobs was to get water and boil it. Azupka, had come with us because he was such a good worker and saw what had to be done. We opened some cans of beans and wieners and vegetables; we also had a gingerbread mix and managed to prepare supper in a short time. We found only one dead mouse—behind Jody's sofa. We were all so exhausted that after supper and a shower, we could think of nothing more welcome than sleep. The next day, Sunday, was to be a busy one.

We were awakened early by the school director's rooster and the chattering of the weaver birds. After we had scurried around to find something for breakfast, the peal of the church bell, halfway down the hill, summoned us to morning service.

The church was filled. Most of the people from the nearby leper colony had also come. How happy everyone was to see not one but two doctors! Each of us gave a short greeting to the people, and Art Zylstra sang a song in Spanish because he had been a missionary to Ecuador. The Congolese were fascinated by Art. He was large in stature, and they couldn't get over his size. They always referred to him as *mondele monene,* the big man.*

For Sunday dinner we had capitani, a delicious whitefish we had bought in the fishing village of Banzyville Saturday on our way up. In a letter home we described that scene: "We wish you could have been along to see the buying of it—it was a scream! Jody did the bargaining, and she is a riot. She found out that the official price was supposed to be 40 francs a kilo. The man wanted 60 francs. The fish weighed 16 kilos, or around 36 pounds. After bartering

---

*Art Zylstra died suddenly of a heart attack on his way home from Alaska in September 1964, the week of Paul's capture by the Simbas.

back and forth (they just don't think it is a good sale unless there is considerable bargaining) and even getting back into the truck and starting the motor to show them we were leaving because we didn't like their price, they finally came down to 50 francs a kilo. We ended up paying about the equivalent of three dollars for 36 pounds of delicious fish. Throughout the bartering session the poor fish was slipping around on the hook-scale. How we would have liked to have a movie camera with sound!"

On Sunday afternoon, Jody and Paul insisted that Art, Fernly, and Ron take a pirogue ride on the Uele River, so with eight rowers they set out for the village on the other side of the river, and from all reports they enjoyed it. The river is so swift that it is necessary to row at a 45-degree angle in order to row straight across. People in the village were so happy to have visitors that they gave them a couple of chickens and some eggs. Paul was too busy to go, but Jody went with them as guide and interpreter. Meanwhile, Paul, Elsie, Lyn, and I were lining up things at Wasolo for work on Monday, which was to be our only workday there. Already many patients were staying in and around the hospital, waiting for the doctor who, they had heard, was coming. Paul was surprised and pleased to know that so many in the area were eagerly waiting for his care—and how impatient we were to get there permanently!

On Monday, which happened to be Labor Day in the States, the doctors performed six operations. One was on a man for a hernia that hung to his knees. He was so grateful to the doctors for coming. Elsie ran the operating room and Jody took care of a million and one things. Lyn and I helped her count out pills and put up medicines for the Congolese nurses there and for the two dispensaries maintained by Wasolo hospital. It was also my job to feed the group.

By nightfall we were thoroughly exhausted, but happy, too, over the accomplishments of the day.

We rose about 4 a.m. Tuesday, had breakfast, packed a road lunch, locked things up, and started out on the long day-trip to Goyongo, so that our visitors could see the Bible institute and seminary. About 9 a.m. we came to a wooden bridge that a road crew was repairing. At that point it was torn out completely, and we could do nothing but wait. It seemed to be the time for morning coffee from our thermos. The workers enjoyed putting on a show of their workmanship for us, and they chanted in rhythm as they handled the heavy logs. In the unbelievably short time of two hours the bridge was crossable and we were on our way.

About noon we stopped in a shady spot for a quick lunch. Then, about three o'clock in the afternoon, as we came to the fork in the road to take us to Goyongo, under some shade trees we saw Frank and Margaret with their daughter Sheri. They had had an errand that way and, knowing we were due along there—nothing is private in the Ubangi, where the only means of communication is by radio—they had brought a chocolate cake and coffee.

We finally arrived at Goyongo somewhat after seven in the evening. There we found that Polly Monson, a Free Church missionary, had an infected ulcer on her leg. The two doctors insisted that she go to bed and stay there, but she had two children—ages two years and six months—and it was decided that Lyn and I should stay with her until one of the nurses could come to be with her. We remained for a week while the other travelers continued on because they had a tight schedule. By the time they returned to Karawa, Dr. Helen Berquist had arrived, and so Paul could devote more time to Lingala study then.

Lyn and I remained at Goyongo until arrangements were made for further care of Polly. About that time, Frank, Margaret, and Sheri had come to Goyongo to bring some Bible-school students and then to take others back to Gbado for classes there. Lyn and I were to travel as far as Gbado with them. What a trip we had! I don't know how many were in the truck, counting all the Congolese students with us. Everything went well until we were about one hour from Gbado, and then, just after dark, a main spring broke and the truck was resting on the back tires. Fortunately, we were only about a mile from a Catholic mission, and so we walked there for shelter for the night. The brothers at the mission couldn't have been more sympathetic and kind to us had they been from our own mission. They insisted that we eat at their table—they had just finished their evening meal. They fixed pancakes with dark brown sugar on them for Lyn and Sheri, who was also with us. Then they put us up in their guest room for the night. There was a little gray angora kitten, which the girls brought into the room, amidst much giggling and laughter. We couldn't shush them, and we feared that they would greatly disturb the brothers. The next morning the brothers assured us that they hadn't heard such happy sounds in their house for a long time. Then they took the girls around and showed them a pet antelope. About the time we were finishing breakfast, Ed Noren, from the Gbado mission, appeared. He had come to look for us. Repairs were made to our truck, and soon we were on our way.

Meanwhile, our disappearance had caused Paul and the others some concern. We did not reach Gbado until noon, when there was a radio call-in to let the others know that we had arrived and what had happened.

This is Nine-Q-Three-One calling, Nine-Q-Three-One... Lindquists, Lois, and Lyn arrived. Truck had broken spring. All is well.... Over.

The message was repeated in five minutes, and then: *Nine-Q-Three-One signing off.... Over and out.*

Finally we were reunited at Karawa, and with Paul now free from hospital cares, we were determined to get our language study out of the way so we could get on to Wasolo and the work that awaited us there.

VI

The Forgotten Corner

Wasolo station is an obscure part of Congo, so remote that it is known as *le coin perdu*, the lost, or forgotten, corner. The way the rivers flow and the jungles grow and the land lies makes Wasolo hard to get to from any direction, even from places that look, on the map, to be within easy distance.

Wasolo lies about 300 miles north of the equator and fifteen miles south of the junction of the three rivers that form the Ubangi, which puts it close to the geographical center of Africa. It is in the extreme northeastern part of Ubangi Province, a region the size of Iowa.

And now the time had come for our move to this forgotten corner. The year of specialized training, first in tropical medicine for Paul and then in French and Lingala for all of us, was behind us. Once more the Carlsons were packing. Wayne would be remaining in Karawa attending Ubangi Academy. Although he would be with us in Wasolo every nine weeks for a two-week vacation, and for two months in the summer, Paul and I were having difficulty getting used to the idea of separation. He was a bit sad, too, at our impending departure, but he was happy to stay with the other children in

Karawa. Lyn would be coming with us, of course, because she was only six— she celebrated her birthday just at the time of our move to Wasolo in October— and missionary children didn't live in the dormitory until they were seven. I would be teaching her first-grade subjects at home.

Moving with us to Wasolo was Azupka and his family. We had grown fond of Azupka during our time at Karawa and were delighted he could come to Wasolo. Actually, he was "on loan" to us for some months while the missionaries for whom he regularly worked were on furlough. Now in his forties, he had worked for missionaries for many years and we found his common sense and ready willingness for work invaluable in the household tasks.

The road seemed to be especially bad at the time we moved and the load in our truck was particularly heavy because we were moving Azupka's belongings as well as our own. When we were still about two hours from Wasolo the clouds gathered and the rains began to pelt down until there was a thunderous downpour that quickly filled all the holes in the road. When it is dry the holes are at least visible, but now with the rain making each hole seem as deep (or as shallow) as any other, we had to move ahead very slowly and carefully. However, by the time we finally drew up in front of the Wasolo hospital, the rain had stopped. The people ran out to meet us and everyone was smiling. Some were calling out in Lingala, "Monganga Paul is here! Monganga Paul is here!"

I could see in his manner how happy Paul was to be back. When he was happy, which was most of the time, he became talkative and so enthusiastic that you found yourself swept along in his plans and sharing in his high spirits. After we had greeted the people we started to drive up the hill. It was perhaps one-half mile to the top. Leading up the hill was a lovely avenue of tall trees that we called Mango Lane. Midway up the hill on the left was the church with its deep red roof and bell tower, and beyond it the pastor's house; across the road, on the right, the school and houses for the teachers and cooks. As we approached the top of the hill we passed between a short avenue of palms. We had been so busy on our brief visit here the month before that I had scarcely had time to see the place. Now, as we reached the top of the hill, I looked around and noticed how overgrown everything was.

"Where's that view you've been talking about so much, Paul?" I asked.

He turned to me with a smile. "Right over here on the east side of the house," he said, motioning with his usual relaxed kind of gesture. My eye followed the direction of his gesture, but all I could see was grass and brush.

"We'll have that cut down, and then you'll see a big difference," he promised. Paul—typically buoyant, energetic, and able to see things that many people could not—could visualize and plan in a way that never failed to impress me. A few weeks later we had workers cut the grass and brush. They thought it was a useless endeavor, but when they had finished, a breathtaking panorama unfolded. Azupka said, "Now I see why the doctor had that cut down." The average Congolese did not seem to see the beauty of nature. To them nature was harsh. The land was difficult to till. Forests had to be roamed for wildlife to kill for meat. Too much or too little rain meant hardship.

We moved quickly toward the house that was to be our home, an attractive reddish brick structure with a dramatic roofline. I could see that it would need a lot of cleaning to make it livable because it had not been occupied for some time, but Paul's enthusiasm was infectious, and I was as excited about being there as he was. Walking up to the entrance and opening the outer screen door, he put his key in the lock and pushed the door open.

The odor that assailed us as we entered the spacious living room was the smell that seemed to typify Congo, a musty smell that would cling to everything—a book, for instance—even years after it had been out of Congo. "And we'll get that woodstove out of the kitchen and into the laundry house," Paul was saying. "The laundry house can become the cookhouse, and that will spare you the extra heat this stove would make in the kitchen." As Paul sensed, another advantage of putting the stove in a separate area was that it would give Azupka a domain of his own, and would increase his feeling of independence and importance.

"This is the living room," he said, referring to the room we had walked into first, and we moved through it to the bedrooms. "And here I thought we would be, and Wayne in here—this was a study—and Lyn can have this room, over here." He motioned to the third room. Then he described how he planned to move the unattractive radio transmitter from the living room into Wayne's room, which also was to be our office, since Wayne would be in school at Karawa most of the time.

How typical this was of Paul! When he saw a new environment, whether house or hospital or church, he began to plan, for he had an innate sense of the best way to arrange things. We were soon settled in our new home and adjusted to life at Wasolo.

In a letter he wrote home during his first visit to Wasolo in 1961, Paul described how he could sit comfortably in the living room of the house and look across the valley to the east into Lumumba territory. By the time we moved to Wasolo, Patrice Lumumba had been dead for some time, but his memory was far from dead. He had been prime minister of the government of Congo just after Belgian rule ended, and within a few months of his rise, the people of Katanga Province, under Moise Tshombé, rebelled against the Lumumba government and civil war broke out. A long period of confusion and widespread fighting ensued, during which the United Nations moved in. Finally, Lumumba was captured and killed, and his followers, considering him a martyr, built a monument to him in Stanleyville where some people would go and pray before his life-sized portrait which formed part of the monument. Many of these people called themselves "Simbas," the Swahili word for lion.

Since independence there had been tension between the Lumumba supporters, who were mostly in north and east Congo, and the supporters of Tshombé, who were in the south and west. By the time we went to Congo, the major problems seemed to have been brought under control. While there had been some scattered violence, we did not feel that there was grave danger in the Ubangi, because United Nations forces remained in Congo as a stabilizing influence.

If the bright green of the leaves and the brilliance of the hibiscus and poinsettia reminded me of the California we had left, there were many other reminders that life at Wasolo was more than a world removed from life in Torrance. The sun rose abruptly at about 6 a.m., and the hour varied little from one month to the next because we were so close to the equator.

We had no need for an alarm clock; if the early sun failed to rouse us, the rattling sound from the cookhouse would. The cookhouse was just back of the kitchen, and Azupka would get an early start by stoking the fire in the old-fashioned wood-burning stove. The iron grates would rattle and the stove lids would clatter as he commenced operations.

No longer was cooking simply a matter of turning dials. The stove, an old country-style model with black iron top and white enamel front and sides, had an oven and, on the right side, a reservoir for keeping water warm. We did have a gas stove, but we used it only occasionally because gas was hard to get. And it wasn't possible to turn on a faucet for water without a thought as to where it was coming from or without considering how soon the gravity-fed tanks would have to be refilled. That, too, presented a problem, and for these reasons there was a good deal to do even before we sat down to breakfast. To heat water we had a large old kettle that sat on top of the wood stove alongside the teakettle and the coffee pot.

To cook food, and to get water in which to cook it, took constant labor. In addition, during the year that we were at the mission we undertook many repair projects because in all the political unrest preceding the time of our arrival, nobody had lived in the house and things had fallen into neglect. In the tropics an uninhabited house becomes uninhabitable more rapidly than in a temperate climate.

Workers were always around the house, including men we had hired and others looking for jobs. They would begin to arrive while we were still dressing and would stand around outside the house, coughing and clearing their throats and talking loudly to make sure we knew they were there. As soon as he was dressed Paul would go out and greet them and talk with them. They were happy to see him, and they would listen as he described the day's projects. He had an unusual warmth of feeling and his obvious liking for people was one of the reasons they responded to him so wholeheartedly.

On a typical day, by the time Paul had organized the men, Azupka would have prepared most of the breakfast. Dressed in his bright red flannel shirt, his shorts, sandals, and knee-length khaki apron, he moved noiselessly. About 5' 8" in height, he was slight of build. As I readied the last-minute things, Paul would sit down with his Bible for a few moments of private prayer and meditation. When the family sat down to the table he would pick up the devotional book we used and read the lesson for the day aloud—a Bible verse, a short meditation, and then as we bowed our heads, he would offer a short prayer:

"Thank you Lord for the privilege of having another day here—another day to work and serve. We pray for guidance for us and for understanding of our Congolese brothers despite cultural differences. Speed our patients to restored health and watch over us as we renew our efforts in healing. Thank you for this food given for the nourishment of our bodies and bless our home and our mission in Jesus' name. Amen."

He always kept his prayers simple because of the children. His language was direct, which made the prayer even more personal and deeply felt than formal language might.

Azupka, who had grown accustomed to our family devotions, stayed outside close to the cookhouse, talking to any of the people who might still be waiting to see Paul, so that we would not be disturbed.

During breakfast we regularly listened to the news through the British Broadcasting Company or the Voice of America. In a remote spot like Wasolo, radio was the principal way to stay in touch with the outside world.

By 7:30 Paul would have finished his breakfast and be on his way to the hospital. To cover the distance down the hill he soon began using a motorbike. Almost every minute of his day had some demand made on it by his duties at the hospital, but with the motorbike he could occasionally take a few minutes from his busy schedule for a cup of coffee with us at the house.

After Paul left for the hospital Lyn and I started lessons and, whenever possible, I combined teaching with some household chore. Often it would be going for water. At the bottom of the hill was a well, but the pump didn't work. According to early plans for Wasolo, this well would supply both the hospital and the dwellings at the top of the hill. The work on it, which had been started just before Congo's independence in 1960, was never finished. The piping and electric pump were there, but not installed. A simple hand pump for temporary use had been put in, but that was broken. Just before evacuation, when Paul took us out of Wasolo, we were trying to get it fixed. In fact, our mission mechanic was working on it, trying to get it in operation before the next dry season, which begins each year in November.

For drinking water we depended on a spring not far from our house. One of the yard workers we hired would "cut water" for us. A dipper scooping into a pool of water is thought of as "cutting" out some water, and that is the way they describe it in Lingala. We filled two-gallon demijohns and then we had to boil the water before using it. The water for kitchen use and baths was kept in fifty-five-gallon metal drums.

Water assumes great importance in Congo. When writing to friends in California, congratulating them on their new baby, I said: "I can imagine the piles of laundry you must have with four children! I hope you appreciate your washer and are thankful for a good water supply. That's what I really miss out here. We have a system of running water in the house, fortunately—several fifty-five-gallon barrels installed under the eaves of the house so that during rainy season they fill up from the water running off the roof; these barrels are connected to a pipe system bringing the water into the kitchen and bathroom for the basin and flush toilet. It works very well except when something clogs with leaves and dirt! During dry season we haul water from the spring and fill this water system. We are hoping by next dry season we can get the well-water system going. I just hate having to skimp on water. We spend so much time getting it. We have to haul for the hospital, too, and I am the chauffeur for this job, so it means three or four trips a week to the water supply with a half-dozen workers and a half-dozen fifty-five-gallon barrels."

Workers would load the big barrels into the back of the truck and I would start off with Lyn and Kanga Joseph, one of our yard workers, riding in front with me. As we reached the hospital area, "Little Joseph" (as we called him because of his stature) would recruit helpers from the people always around there. They were relatives of the patients, who had come in with the sick to prepare their food and to help care for them, as is the custom in Congo. They were eager to earn a little money. We had to charge for medicine or we couldn't have maintained our supply and there was a small fee for hospital care, so any extra money these relatives could pick up by helping us found a ready use.

The men enlisted by Little Joseph clambered into the back of the truck and we drove on to the stream, which was fed by springs. The water bubbled from the ground at its source into a kind of basin, hollowed out of the slight rise in the land, that was about fifteen feet across and one or two feet deep. The bed was light-colored sand with a scattering of small stones and gravel and the water was so clear that you could see the springs gushing up underneath, as if they were garden hoses pushing bubbling water out from underneath. Around the edges of the basin ferns sprang up and behind these ferns dense forest completely surrounded the little pond. It was a lovely cool spot in which to spend an hour; the sun made patterns through the leaves overhead onto the clear water's surface. Insects made their chorus of humming and buzzing. Birds whistled and called. The metal tubs clattered against the barrels and the sound of the men loading the demijohns and filling the great drums came welling up. I suppose Lyn didn't always appreciate it as much as I, because, pleasant as it was, to her it was an open-air classroom.

As we sat in the truck, going through her lessons, other people coming down for water would stop when they heard Lyn reading aloud or saw her doing problems. As they watched, their interest increased and they would begin to whisper and gesture among themselves about the little girl who was able to learn. I like to think that the sight of Lyn may have had some influence on them to change their way of thinking, because they believed that girls and women couldn't learn. That was one reason why there were so few girls in school.

When the workers were done they piled into the truck and I drove up to the house where the men poured the water into the barrels that made up our gravity-fed system for the shower and the sinks in the house. On the next trip, in a day or so, we'd get water for the hospital.

Inside the house Lyn and I went on with her lessons. That was the time of day when women stopped by on their way from their gardens with bananas, papaya, corn, squash, peanuts, and other fruits and vegetables, or with chickens and eggs, for sale. I always left change in the kitchen drawer for Azupka so he could take care of the routine purchases, but he would often call me to consult about them. He took care of most of the preparations for the noon meal but I made dessert with Lyn helping me. She enjoyed mixing cakes and cookies as I measured out the ingredients.

After that there was still time left for sewing. I made Lyn's and my own clothes. So, with buying fruit and vegetables and eggs from the women who came by and with cooking and sewing, Lyn's morning of lessons ended as a home economics class. By then, Paul and Jody, who had moved back to Wasolo now that we were there, would be coming in for lunch exhausted from a busy morning of surgery and making rounds in the hospital.

Usually, Paul's first question was, "What happened on radio this morning?"

"Folks in Gbado are taking Sheri to Karawa to see Dr. Helen."

"What happened to Sheri?"

"She was hit in the eye."

"By what?"

"A stone from a slingshot."

"Is it bad?"

"They're concerned. She had some bleeding so they wanted Dr. Helen to take a look."

Paul took a bite of his lunch. "I hope she'll be all right."

"Gemena was asking somebody from Tandala to try to get some intravenous fluid," I continued. The government hospital at Gemena had suffered from erratic shipments of drugs since independence.

"Doesn't Gemena even have fluids?"

"I don't know. They're asking Tandala for them for some patient." Paul looked concerned, frowned a bit, and shook his head. I could tell how much he was troubled by the inadequate treatment that so many people, even in hospitals better equipped than Wasolo, suffered. At all of these hospitals, the ratio of doctors to patients was about 1 to 100,000.

On a typical day, more than 200 patients would require attention at Wasolo. Paul was often weary by noontime after nearly five hours of intensive work, and I tried to make it possible for him to have a long, uninterrupted rest, especially when he had been up late the night before on an emergency.

He believed that we ought to conserve our health and our energy. Paul said more than once that he was convinced that missionaries in the tropics who did not take care of themselves by such things as midday siestas in the heat of the day did not last out their term. Whenever it was possible he rested, but it often turned out that a real rest was not possible. There would be a crisis that required him to return to the hospital while the heat of midday was still upon us. Whether there was a crisis or not, however, Paul went back to the hospital in the afternoon to see his patients from the surgery of that morning, to check temperatures, and to continue making rounds of the other patients.

A day that stands out clearly in my mind is the one I have come to think of as "The Day of the Wild Pig."

Meat is scarce in the Ubangi region. We did not always have it on our table and the Congolese seldom had meat as part of their diet. They suffered protein deficiency, and because of that they would often take risks when hunting.

It was the stillness of midday. We had eaten our lunch and now it was siesta time. The sun sat high overhead, the jungles throbbed with the sounds of insect life, and the steam from the moist earth fairly hung in the air while many small bugs buzzed at the screen in the kitchen window. Paul had been up late the night before because of an emergency. He had operated three times that morning and had seen probably a hundred patients besides. Now he was sleeping, and I was hopeful that he could enjoy a long rest.

I was crossing the breezeway between the kitchen and the cookhouse when I suddenly became aware of a commotion on the other side of the house. Just then a Congolese sprang into view around the corner. He was pumping excitedly on his bicycle and as he neared the breezeway, he leaped off, ran to me, and began talking excitedly.

"Madame Docteur," he said, puffing and gulping for breath, "we need the doctor to come with the truck and get my friend. He's hurt—very bad." This was in Lingala, and he went on with great speed, pouring out many words that I didn't understand. I was not sure the crisis was as great as he seemed to be painting it, and I didn't want to disturb Paul unless it was absolutely necessary.

Paul made a rule when he first arrived that all patients who came to the hospital while he was off duty should be examined first by the Congolese nurse who was on duty. If Paul's presence was required, the nurse would then send for him. So I asked the man to bring a note from the nurse if Paul was needed. I turned back to my tasks in the kitchen, thinking of what had happened and wondering if I had done the right thing. I finished putting the dishes on the shelf, and snapped the door closed. Just about that time the Congolese was back, still huffing from the ride up the hill, and as excited as before. As I looked at the note and saw his gestures become more emphatic and heard his talk grow more excited, I suddenly knew in my heart that the case was urgent.

His friend had been hunting. A wild pig had charged him and, with the fearsome tusks those animals have, had ripped into the Congolese hunter and torn him open. Other members of the hunting party had made a sling carrier for their wounded comrade by tying the ends of a fishing net to a pole, and two of them had started carrying him to the hospital in it. They sent the third man ahead on his bicycle to ask that the mission truck come out and meet them. That man was now standing in front of me imploring me to get the doctor.

Feeling terrible that so much time had been lost, I rushed in and called Paul, who quickly dashed out and jumped into the mission truck with the Congolese. I heard the sound of the truck as it bumped down Mango Lane and out of earshot.

By now, of course, the peace of siesta had been shattered. In all the hub-bub Jody had been alerted and had gone down to the hospital to be on hand when they brought the man in. Meantime, I had to get ready for the twenty girls who would be arriving at two o'clock for a sewing class. These girls were third-to sixth-grade students in the Wasolo mission school. They eagerly looked forward to the sewing class three afternoons a week. We met in a spare room in Jody's duplex. (We always referred to Jody's house as the duplex. Originally it had been built to house two single women.) As there were no sewing machines, I was teaching the girls hand sewing. At this point they were growing impatient with me because they had to piece together little scraps of material to make a patchwork pillow. This seemed to me the best way for them to learn the different kinds of stitches before going on to more difficult things like skirts and blouses. Of course, they were much more interested in making something to wear, as most girls their age would be, and they had the impatience of young

The Carlson family in 1947 (from left to right): Paul in his Navy uniform, Ruth, Sharon, Gust, and Dwight

The Carlson family before leaving for Congo in 1962 (from left to right): Wayne, Lynette, Lois, and Paul

Paul, Lois, and children with their dog, "Lady" in front of their home in Wasolo. This picture was taken in May 1964, three months before the deteriorating political situation in Congo forced the Carlsons to evacuate.

Paul and other doctors receive gifts of eggs, corn, and chicken in appreciation of their visit to a village.

Enjoying homemade root beer in the Carlsons' front yard (facing camera, left to right): Philip Littleford, medical student from Johns Hopkins Medical School, in Congo for several months' field work on a Smith, Kline & French fellowship; Jody LeVahn, mission nurse assigned to the Wasolo hospital; Paul; Lois; Lyn; and Wayne

Saying a prayer before their meal (from left to right): Lyn; Wayne (partially hidden); Paul; Lois; Philip Littleford; Dr. Robert Etherington; Elsie Carlson (no relation); Mark Enos (visible in mirror); and Kurt Lindquist, Paul's nephew

Wasolo hospital

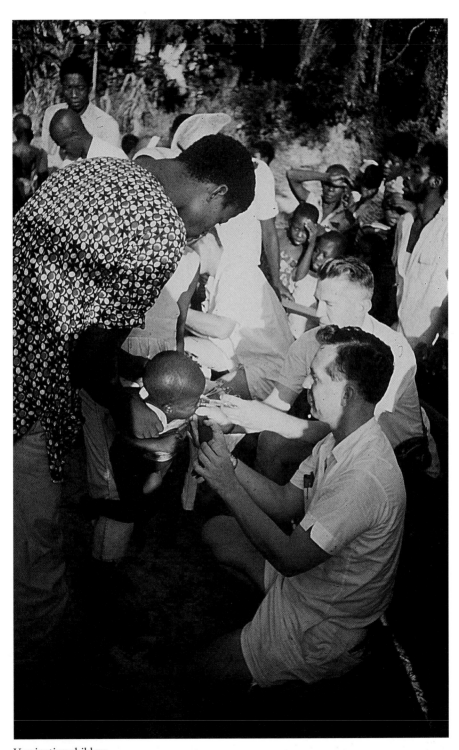

Vaccinating children

Paul, Wayne, and others travel to the village of Dongbe in a dugout canoe (a pirogue).

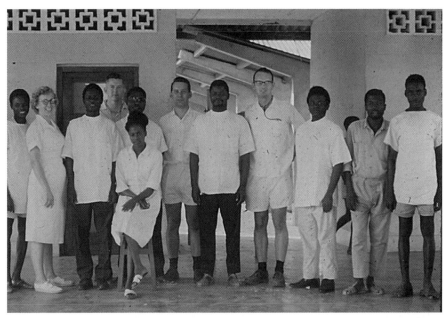

Wasolo hospital staff (left to right, starting from second person): Jody LeVahn; Bomba Boniface, nurse; Dr. Bob Etherington; Ndikini, nurse; Flossie Bangi, midwife; Dr. Paul Carlson; Wanzi, nurse; Philip Littleford, visiting medical student; and (extreme right) Constant Kokembe, hospital worker. Boniface and Kokembe were later killed when Simbas appeared unexpectedly at Wasolo and forced Paul to drive them in the mission truck to Targini.

The operating room at Wasolo hospital. Nurse Wanzi (foot of the table), Paul and Bob Etherington prepare for surgery as Nurse Elsie Carlson administers ether to a patient.

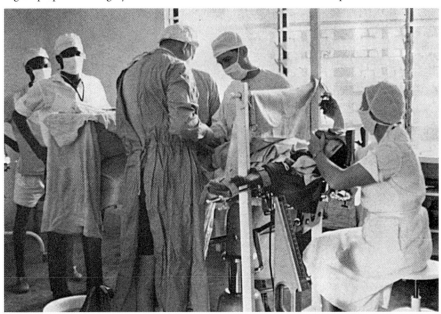

A person too ill to walk to Wasolo hospital (often a one- or two-day hike from a remote village) would be carried in by friends.

Outpatient clinic at Wasolo hospital

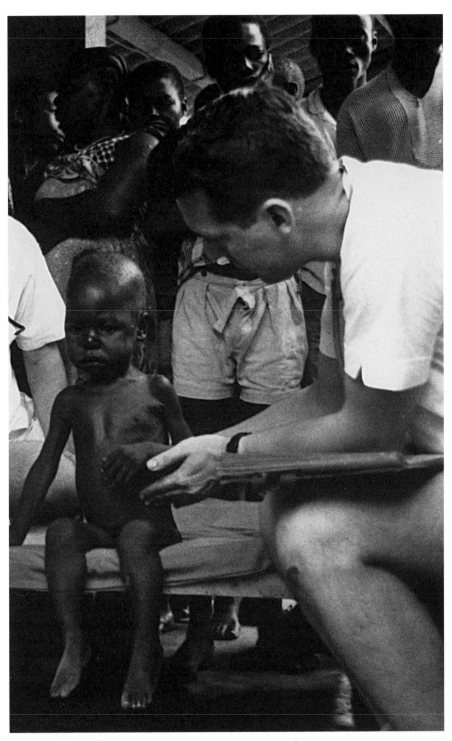

Paul evaluates a child.

Wedding of Flossie Bangi, midwife, and Paul Sedua shortly before the Carlsons evacuated

Wasolo church after the morning service. Flossie (extreme right) and Paul Sedua's wedding was held here.

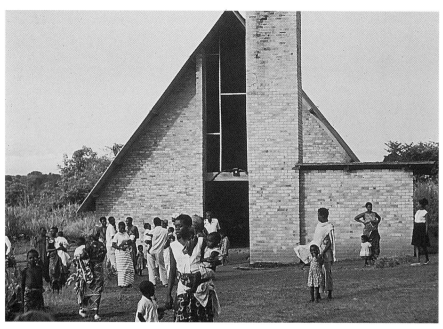

Christophe Gbenye, leader of the Simba rebellion

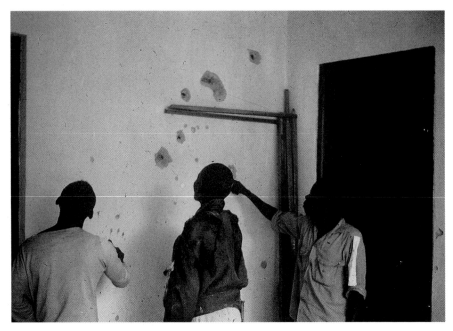

Rebel bullets left their scars in the wall of Wasolo hospital.

Bob Thornbloom talks on the radio with Paul Carlson, while Paul was trapped at Wasolo in early September 1964. Missionary Frank Lindquist is standing nearby.

Paul and other hostages surrounded by rebel soldiers

(From left to right) Paul Carlson; Jon Snyder, Mennonite conscientious objector; Michael Hoyt, U.S. consul; and other hostages listen as Simba leader Gbenye announces Paul's imminent execution.

U.S. Air Force planes carried paratroopers for the November 24 rescue attempt.

Belgian paratroopers on the way to Congo

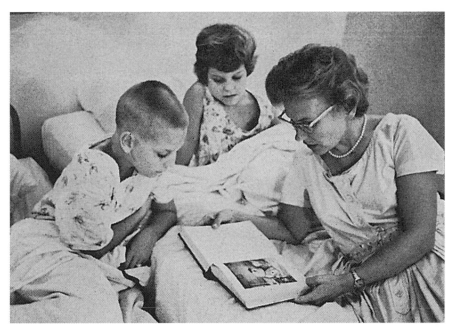

Lois reads to Wayne and Lyn while waiting for word about Paul.

Paul Carlson's grave in Karawa. On the marker is the verse John 15:13 in Lingala.

The December 4, 1964 issue of *Time* magazine covered the story of Dr. Paul Carlson and the massacre in Congo. This copy carries the signature of Paul's father, Gust Carlson.

people everywhere with the slowness of learning. They had trouble getting used to the idea that to do something well necessitates starting at the beginning and proceeding step by step.

They were a cheerful, lively group, laughing and chattering and joking, and were fun to be with, so the hour and a half passed quickly. As the months progressed, so did their skill and they made skirts and blouses and even panties and bras. These latter items brought great delight when I let them trim them with lace which had been given to me by a neighbor in California. I hoped as I became more fluent in Lingala to be able to teach them more about homemaking, etiquette, and morals. I realized that someday these girls from "the forgotten corner" might be marrying persons with education, possibly living in a city, thus making it necessary for them to know social graces and housekeeping on a different level from what they were accustomed to.

As soon as class was over on that particular day I hurried down to the hospital and went right into the operating room. Paul was still at work over the man, and busy suturing alongside him was the Congolese nurse and hospital administrator, Wanzi. My nursing experience told me that, despite the extent of his injuries, the wounded man seemed to be in fair condition.

I learned from Paul later that right after the pig attacked the unfortunate fellow, his friends gathered around and someone had just the right idea of how to protect him and his terrible wounds. They placed banana leaves, which are large and broad and somewhat moist by nature, across the open abdomen and then tied the leaves firmly with a vine. This moist covering kept the intestines from drying and the firmly tied vine held the parts together, especially during the jouncing ride in the sling, and later in the rear of the truck when Paul drove him to the hospital. Fortunately, the internal organs, as Paul found upon examination, had not been injured.

Wanzi was always Paul's right-hand man in surgery. He had a deep respect for Paul, and Paul was just as grateful for Wanzi's faithfulness and loyalty and willingness to be on call at almost any time of night or day. Whenever an emergency arose at the hospital requiring Paul's presence, Wanzi would be on the scene too. He would rush from his house, which was just across the road from the hospital, as Paul rushed down from our house. Paul sometimes thought that emergency calls were less wearing on Wanzi than bill-collecting. As hospital administrator, he had to collect the small fees asked of the patients. He knew the hospital had to have money; he knew his fellow Congolese had almost no money. It was a difficult situation for him.

Now as I looked on in the operating room, Wanzi was busy with the large, nasty tear on the man's thigh, sewing carefully but swiftly. Meantime, Paul was bent over the man's hand, where the suturing had to be more precise and the stitches closer together, if the hand was to be restored to full usefulness. Naomi Skoglund had often remarked on Paul's skill and swiftness, and his abilities as a surgeon rested in no small part on his precision with the surgical needle.

By this time, Paul and Wanzi had been working for several hours on the man gored by the pig. The afternoon was wearing on and the weariness that Paul felt after his late night the night before, three operations that morning, and then this exhausting operation this afternoon, began to tell. They were both eager to finish before dusk because the diesel plant at the hospital was not working properly then, and to continue after dark would mean that they would have to work by lantern light. Paul gave me a nod that all was going well as I slipped out of the operating room and went on up the hill to start the light plant there.

Supper preparations seemed well under way by the cook at Jody's, where we were to eat that evening, so I went on to our house. The sun was near the horizon and I listened for a moment to the sounds of late afternoon. The weaver birds never seemed to stop their chattering in the large tree close by. The light plant was thumping properly. A gentle breeze was rustling the leaves. All seemed calm and peaceful.

Paul came in just after dusk and Jody was with him. They were both tired, but also both were clearly satisfied with the day's work. I could tell that without asking.

Lyn was just as anxious as I was to hear about the man's chances for getting well. So now she followed our conversation closely—just the way, I imagine, Paul followed grown-up conversations closely when he was Lyn's age. Paul said he thought the man's chances were good, mainly because there had been no damage to his internal organs. Even though the pig had caught him directly with his tusks and had ripped a deep, large, and extremely dirty wound in his abdomen, still, miraculously, no serious damage had been done to any organ. The principal danger was infection from the dirtiness of the wound. Of course I was greatly relieved that the delay I had caused had not been the difference between life and death. Later the man recovered fully, the only complication being a small stitch abscess.

After supper at Jody's that night we returned to our house for the showers we would have taken earlier if Paul had not had to work so late at the hospital. Then we settled down for one of our typical Congo evenings. In the background was the thudding of the diesel motor, which pulsated through the evening, a constant reminder that we were dependent on that machinery for light and power to run our radio transmitter and receiver. Occasionally we might worry a little that it would get out of order.

Some people think of missionaries as completely solemn people, and I confess that as a child I used to think a missionary was someone with a bun in her hair and a grave manner incapable of having any fun. But it wasn't like that at Wasolo. We were all fond of music, for instance, and we had a good tape recorder which Paul turned on as soon as the light plant went on. Lyn and Paul both loved to play games, and they were often part of the evening's activities. Frequently Jody would spend the evening at our house for the company or to make some hospital reports and do some writing. By eight or so, it was time for Lyn to go to bed. I would read to her from her favorite book, Egermeier's *Bible Story Book*, and then, after bedtime prayer, we tucked her in and said goodnight.

While Paul wrote the letters that he was always so conscientious about writing, I would take advantage of the electric current and do some sewing. One of my projects was to make curtains for the examining room and offices at the hospital to replace the tattered ones hanging there. To peer into examining rooms was a most interesting diversion for the Congolese, but was not enjoyed by the patients or the doctor. Jody's solution to the problem was as effective as curtains, though. She had planted cacti beneath the window of the operating room.

Often during the evening, Florence Bangi, daughter of our Congolese pastor, Matthieu Bangi, would drop in. Slender, twenty-year-old Flossie was a lovely Christian who became one of our dearest friends. She had been educated at the mission school, and had trained as a midwife at Karawa hospital. Now as the midwife at Wasolo hospital, she took care of most of the maternity cases.

One evening each week we invited the school children to our house for a sing-time. The people of the Wasolo area loved to sing so this was enjoyed immensely accompanied with our small organ. Paul sang enthusiastically—often going off key! The singing was interspersed with a Bible quiz or game. Sometimes the sing-time ended with a treat of popcorn or homemade peanut brittle.

Paul believed in keeping our church people in the United States informed about our activities and one time he wrote a short article entitled "Your Day in Congo" for the newspaper of one of our supporting churches. In it he captured better than I have how it felt to be the doctor at a place like Wasolo:

If you were awakened today by a billy goat chasing a bellowing nanny goat in your yard or screeching weaver birds in the tree outside your window, or the church bell for morning chapel at 5:30 a.m.—you might know you had awakened in the Congo, or, to pinpoint it more, Wasolo. You awake to an unpredictable day, of that you can be certain. At least you can be thankful you weren't awakened as you were two nights ago by the night sentry in tattered pants with a long spear. He had had a note from the night nurse asking you to see a baby with meningitis, who had just come in. Upon seeing him you found that he had been given Congolese medicine in the village for three days, but his parents waited until he became critical at three in the morning before coming to the hospital.

You hear the truck and remember that your nurse, Jody LeVahn, is going to make a trip out to get some rocks for the base of the floor of the new ward that is being remodeled. If she goes out now she'll be back before the first patients arrive at the dispensary.

You pause for your morning devotions, and then breakfast, listening with one ear to the world news on BBC from London.

Then hop on your motorbike—down the long hill to the hospital—past the pastor's house and the modern brick church with its impressive red roof—past the school where classes are already in session. The market place at the hospital by now is bustling with early morning bartering. But not a nurse is to be found. And you told them just yesterday to be sure to be here by 7 a.m. so that the temperatures could be taken prior to your making rounds. Sit down for a few minutes; it doesn't pay to get any extra gray hairs over such a little thing.

Your Congolese hospital administrator–head nurse and you make rounds. In the medical ward first, the teenage boy with hemoglobin of only 20 percent who looks as if he had been blown up with the helium gas used for balloons at the circus, except the skin on his legs is like old dried peeling leather. Past the rest of the medical patients to the surgical ward and the chief's wife recovering from surgery for a strangulated hernia. You had thought it would be a relatively easy operation, but the intestine was gangrenous, and while you were removing it, the sun set. The fellow who usually turns on the generator for the emergency lights had gone, as it was Saturday afternoon.* You thought you would use the kerosene lamp, but as Jody brought it down to the hospital the last wick broke. Oh, well, the flashlight didn't work too badly.

There is the man who keeps pushing his hernia out so it will get stuck and you will have to operate on him sooner than his turn. It's kind of rough that you are six weeks behind in your surgery schedule, but one person can't do it all. Past the boy with abdomen filled with cancer; the family wants you to operate, but it would just increase his suffering. To the private room and the young girl who was too little to deliver her baby. She delivered at another dispensary before you arrived at Wasolo, but the poor girl was injured beyond normal repair. You've done one operation to help her, but it wasn't successful. You'll just have to try again.

---

*The hospital generator was particularly tricky and difficult to start. It seemed to require a certain knack to coax it into operation.

To the "Ndako na kelekpa" (house of wooden beds), as the nurses call it. It's an emergency overflow building, repaired and painted up last fall when the 50 beds you had in the hospital were overflowing and something urgent had to be done. You see the patients there and then go back through the medical building, the administration building dispensary area, then to the maternity and children's ward.

First to see the small isolation room, crammed with children with complications of whooping cough—mainly pneumonia. Sounds like a virtual chicken farm. Then the regular children's ward. Except for the meningitis case in the private room, the children seem to be doing well today.

And then maternity! How is the woman doing, whom you operated on late last evening, who came in with a ruptured uterus? Doing well, except for pain and fever, but that's to be expected.

But before you can do more you hear a car come. The Catholic sisters! That means a bad case or they wouldn't travel the dirt roads to come. Another woman with a ruptured uterus! You examine her. No blood pressure, pulse 180, only semiconscious, but enough so still to have terrible pain. History: She spent two days in the village with pain and then two days in coming, having ridden roads for 85 miles in the back of trucks and had to stay overnight at the Catholic mission, as they didn't want to drive in the middle of the night! Do her under local anesthesia, of course! Start the lights! Get an intravenous going if you can find a vein! You look to be sure she is still alive, and pause to pray together before making the incision. The uterus is ripped, most of the baby is in the abdomen outside the uterus. You are giving her drugs to raise her blood pressure—it's up to 40 now—Jody can occasionally feel it. You finish, exhausted. You wonder if you're only going through an exercise, or might she live? Only God knows. Yes, tell her husband the total cost for the surgery, drugs and hospitalization is $2. Oh, he doesn't have it? Maybe one of his relatives will.

Most of the morning is gone. The dispensary patients haven't been seen yet, and there is one of the Portuguese traders here wanting quick care. Jody will finish seeing the patients while you see some of the new problem cases. Then just a few minutes while some of the patients pay you for medicines received. You wish you could just give it to them, as often having to pay 5 or 10 cents is a hardship, but at present there is no other way to get money to buy more medicine.

Noon and dinner. What was the latest news on the shortwave radio stations between our mission stations this morning? Oh, there was too much interference, well maybe tomorrow. Lois also went to the spring this morning, as we were out of water. That means driving to the spring and having barrels loaded with water. After that she had first-grade class for Lyn.

A few minutes of siesta until the school girls are outside for Lois's sewing class. Why can't they wait until two o'clock? But they don't have watches, do they?

Back you go to the hospital to see that everything is still OK—check afternoon temps and look over your notes for a medical teaching session in French for the nurses. But that will wait until tomorrow. It's been a long enough day, and there is still medicine to help give out to the nurses for each of the wards and the last-minute evening checks on patients in poor condition.

It was a hot and dry afternoon. Oh, that shower will feel good. Then a light supper interrupted only by the cat wanting to come in and someone at the door wanting to buy an envelope. It would be fun to relax after supper, but there are hospital books to be done and a stack of letters to be answered.

To refresh the spirit, the tape recorder is on—"Day by day and with each passing moment, strength I find to meet my trials here. . . ." And as you go out to turn the light plant off at 9 p.m. you look across the Congo skies and see a little campfire still lit down by the hospital, reminding you to breathe a prayer of thanks that you could have spent a day here—to breathe a prayer of thanks for the medical work in Congo. Pain was relieved, a life saved, and another chance gained to let someone else know of Christ.

VII

"No One Ever Comes to Wasolo"

"If I had fried that scrawny chicken, and taken a picture of it on the platter on our Thanksgiving table, people back home would really think we are 'poor missionaries.'" Thus I wrote to my parents, describing our holiday at Wasolo. The evening before, I had asked Kanga Joseph to kill one of the chickens for our dinner the next day. After finishing the task, he put the chicken in the refrigerator, and I failed to check on it until time for dinner preparations Thanksgiving morning.

"Why that won't even make good soup!" Azupka exclaimed when he saw it. I asked Joseph why he had killed such a small chicken.

"Because I couldn't catch any other, Madame," he answered. Azupka and I merely shook our heads. Just like Joseph, trying to be helpful, meaning well, but always taking the easy way out. So our mean rooster was chosen instead, and provided a bountiful meal for Paul, Lyn, Jody, and myself. The day was completely ordinary. Paul and Jody had intended to take the afternoon off, but the work load at the hospital did not permit it.

Shortly before Christmas, Paul, Lyn, and I made the long trip to Bangui to pick up some of our personal belongings, shipped from the States many months before, that we had assumed were lost. Among the things in the barrels were Christmas decorations, so our home looked festive with a silvered tree sparkling with colored lights.

Paul wrote his mother about this time: "The next day [after our return from Bangui] was Sunday, and after church we unpacked more things from our barrels. That evening we took about twenty-five sixth graders and folks from here and caroled in the hospital, and then down to the leper colony, trudging single-file through the forest along the little path with our pressure lantern, singing. We were going to another village, but we met a truck bringing someone ill, so I went back to take care of him and the others went on."

Paul always liked to share the holidays with people and, having been alone at Thanksgiving, we invited two missionaries at Karawa, Elsie Carlson and Ann Berg, to spend Christmas with us. They happily accepted our invitation because they enjoyed coming to Wasolo, but of course, no one made such a long and uncomfortable trip except for a specific reason.

Paul's letter to his mother continued: "Christmas Eve day—Elsie, Ann and Wayne arrived from Karawa to spend Christmas with us—many things to fix—we had potato sausage [a traditional Swedish dish]. The casings Mom sent came. Just got enough potatoes for one meal, but did enjoy that plus meatballs, some sardines and sausage brought from Bangui, bread baked with molasses to give the *limpa* flavor [Swedish rye bread], carrot pudding, avocado, grapefruit, Jello, and crab salad, so you see we didn't starve. Then rice pudding, cookies, and coffee bread. But before we could enjoy this, there was an autopsy to be done on a person who died under strange circumstances Sunday. He had been buried for two days, but they had unearthed him for our efforts—equipped with things to improve the smells [to help disguise unpleasant odors, a common practice was to crush a pungent leaf and insert it into one's nostrils]. We did it in an old building of mud. Not quite the way we would at home, but so life goes."

Just as Paul was preparing to go to the late afternoon service on Christmas Eve, he saw white-clad figures approaching the house in the half-light of dusk.

"Why these must be some of the girls from school dressed up like angels for the Christmas play they are giving," he said. But as the figures came closer through the gloom of dusk, they proved to be Catholic sisters from one of the missions in our area, arriving at our door with a patient for surgery. It was a frequent type of case—strangulated hernia of several days' duration. After the service, Paul operated. By then it was dark. The hospital light plant would not start. Our pressure lantern had not survived the evening of caroling. A Coleman lantern and an Aladdin lamp were pressed into service. The patient's chance for survival would diminish greatly if the operation were delayed until morning. Already, Paul knew, the intestine was gangrenous, and would need to be resected. The patient was dehydrated, but not seriously enough to warrant giving the precious dwindling supply of intravenous fluid.

While the patient was being prepared for the operation, our hospital chaplain, Vuku, in mask and gown, sat on a stool near the patient, comforting him in his own tribal language. Vuku had been selected by the pastors of the region, the Wasolo hospital staff, and Paul to serve as chaplain to give spiritual help to the sick. The work of this humble, sincere Christian as hospital chaplain was invaluable. We had found that when our patients were very ill or troubled, they always expressed themselves best in their tribal language, which was their first language. Vuku could speak the tribal language of most of the people who came to our hospital. Not only did he comfort surgical patients before their operations; he was always in the operating room with them during the surgery.

Paul and Wanzi were gloved and ready. Chaplain Vuku offered a short prayer for wisdom for those operating and for strength for the patient. Paul inserted the needle for the spinal anesthetic.

The lamps cast irregular light and shadow on the operative field. In an effort to offset this, Constant Kokembe, one of our most loyal hospital helpers, always available at any hour of the day or night, held a flashlight, supposedly directing the beam into the incision Paul had made, but missing it by several inches. I was standing by and I mentioned something to Paul in English about his "spotlight." Good-naturedly he nodded, "He's trying hard." However Kokembe's attention was brought closer to the situation. The operation proceeded. The lamps proved to be almost overbearingly warm for Paul and Wanzi, and beads of perspiration glistened on their foreheads. I nodded to Paul that the patient's blood pressure held at a normal range, although respiration was rapid.

Meanwhile, Jody had been called to maternity, where our midwife, Flossie, was having difficulty with a delivery. What a night! Soon Jody appeared in the operating room to tell us that mother and child were doing fine, but that the delivery had been very difficult, made even more so because the only light available was from flashlight.

Paul, at this time, was finishing what had turned out to be an extensive intestinal resection. This patient had had a hernia, or rupture, for many years, but there were few, if any, doctors near him during his life, so nothing had been done. He, as all the others do, had lived with it, and it had not given him any particular trouble except for the fact that year after year the size of the hernia sack increased, due to the strain of the man's work, when more intestine had been pushed into it. Only as the growth becomes sufficiently cumbersome to make walking uncomfortable or, as in this patient's case, when a portion of intestine is pinched, cutting off the normal intestinal flow or blood supply, do they come in for surgery.

This patient lived in a remote village without transportation, so he had been carried for two days by his friends until they reached the Catholic mission, where the sisters brought him into Wasolo. By the conclusion of the operation, Paul and Wanzi were weary. The patient was in fair postoperative condition, so I hurried out from the operating room, quickly climbed into the mission truck, and drove up the hill to our house to make a thermos of coffee for the operating-room staff.

Then for all of us came a welcome time of sleep, but it was not many hours before we awakened to Christmas Day. Christmas at Wasolo was as exciting to the children as Christmas anywhere else had ever been.

Paul had been asked to give the Christmas message at the morning church service. He was determined to deliver it in Lingala, and had laboriously prepared it and gone over it with Jody and with Gebanga Joseph, a primary school teacher at Wasolo school. Gebanga Joseph, like his older brother, Wanzi, had become one of our best friends at Wasolo. Tall, slender, always cheerful and with a large, flashing smile, he was one of the best-educated people at Wasolo, having received his schooling in mission schools to the highest level available in Congo. Gebanga Joseph spoke some English, so Lyn always referred to him as "English Joseph," or sometimes "Big Joseph," to distinguish him from "Little Joseph," our yard worker, Kanga Joseph, who was of medium height.

Paul's Christmas message, his first speech in Lingala, went well. Joseph interpreted it into Mongbandi, the local tribal language, because there were so many women and children at the service who did not understand Lingala.

Finally, after the service, we could relax and enjoy the day with our guests, Ann and Elsie. The schoolchildren put on an exhibition of athletics, games, and dances, which was particularly enjoyed by Lyn and Wayne. We celebrated a very different Christmas, but even though we were thousands of miles from America, Santa did not forget us.

Ann and Elsie returned to Karawa within a few days, but Wayne had a three-week vacation from school. This was his first stay at Wasolo, and he quickly became acquainted with Pastor Bangi's sons—Flossie's brothers—of which there were several, as the children in the Bangi family numbered twelve. The boys had such a good time fishing in the stream, riding bicycles, and exploring that we wondered if Wayne would want to return to Karawa. When the time came, however, he was happy to join his school chums again.

After Wayne's return to school, Lyn continued with her lessons at home. Days fell into somewhat of a pattern, although nothing was routine; routine was never possible, even with just Jody, Paul, Lyn, and me. Paul was happy to be almost caught up with the list of patients waiting for surgery. The fifty-bed hospital continued to overflow with a daily census of sixty to ninety patients. In addition, of course, the relatives of the patients were there to help care for them.

At this point, we received the urgent call to Tandala, described earlier, occasioned by Dr. Warren Berggren's grave illness. With the Berggrens leaving Congo, another problem arose. Dr. Warren had promised to sponsor a senior medical student from Johns Hopkins Medical School, under the terms of a fellowship granted by Smith, Kline & French Laboratories. By the time we knew that Dr. Warren would have to leave Congo, the student was already on his way for his several-months stay at Tandala. Warren asked Paul if he would be willing to take the responsibility, because the student had to have a sponsor in order to remain. Paul said he would be very happy to do so.

Paul accompanied the Berggrens to Leopoldville, and while there, was able to meet the medical student, Philip Littleford. Together, they started out for the Ubangi. Finally one day we got the news on radio from Gemena that they had arrived there and would soon be proceeding to Wasolo. Jody and I joked with each other that we didn't know which of us would be happier to see Paul. Jody had the heavy responsibilities of the hospital, and of course Lyn and I were eager to see Daddy again.

Paul and Phil arrived late one afternoon, tired and very muddy. Phil had been properly initiated—the truck got stuck in a mudhole. He was a little embarrassed to meet strangers in such condition, but in typical Congo style, I said, "This is usual, and the shower is right in here."

Phil was to live with us. Lyn moved into Wayne's room temporarily and let Phil have her "rosebud" room, as she called it, because the bedspread had roses on it. Paul was happy to have Phil there. He always enjoyed company, and he was glad to show Phil the hospital, to show him the things we were trying to do as well as the things still needing to be done.

At first Phil was very upset with conditions in the hospital. He had just come from a modern, clean hospital in Baltimore, and Wasolo hospital was not quite what he was used to. The walls in the hospital had been painted recently, but the Congolese routinely wiped their hands on the walls.

"Couldn't we put up some signs asking them not to do this?" Phil wanted to know. We explained to him that most of our patients couldn't read. Even sheets couldn't be kept white, much less the walls. The patients walked about in their bare feet and then climbed into bed, so of course mud stains appeared on the sheets and they were hard to remove. The operating room was kept as clean possible, but still not to the standard that one would like to have. Things were scrubbed and sterilized, and Paul and Jody were constantly after the staff to do a better job, but this all took time. Phil quickly learned that one accepted certain matters, and within two weeks, things were beginning to look cleaner to him than they had on his arrival. We were not lowering our standards—Paul was very meticulous on that point—but everything was very different looking, no matter what we did.

Phil had just finished his laboratory training in medical school, and Paul was delighted to be able to turn over problems in the laboratory at Wasolo to him, hoping that Phil would come up with ideas for improving laboratory techniques and tests under conditions prevailing at Wasolo. Phil proved to be an expert at this, and Paul was pleased with the results that were beginning to come from his work. Phil was also trying to teach the Congolese nurse who worked in the laboratory some new procedures.

Phil took a special interest in the children coming in for treatment. He was eager to learn Lingala, and as soon as he had acquired some vocabulary, he talked to the people in their language as much as he could. When he ran blood tests on some of the children, however, he was appalled at the results. In one instance, after doing a hemoglobin, he turned to Paul, saying, "Well, the book says that this hemoglobin level is incompatible with life."

Paul chuckled. "We find much that is incompatible with life here, Phil."

Paul was also happy to have an extra pair of hands in surgery and to have someone with whom he could discuss problems. Despite the many frustrations in the work, Paul was generally good-natured about things as they went along. He had found out how to cope with many inadequacies in the equipment, but in his mind he was always thinking how things could be done better. Better ways to get the equipment that he needed, and above all, ways to get medicines. He always felt that it was not worth a doctor's time being in Congo if he could not get the necessary medicines. The cost of buying and shipping medicines was unbelievably high. In an effort to arouse interest in the problem, he decided to write an appeal to be sent to our church people in California. It began: "Can you spare a dime, Buddy?" This phrase, reminiscent of the depression years, today would be, "Have you an extra tranquilizer?—or a bottle of aspirin?" Naturally you do. Everyone in North America has more medicine in the medicine cabinet than safety allows. But can you spare it?

Your medicine cabinet may be overloaded while millions of people in Congo don't even have an aspirin to bring down the fever from a death-gripping attack of malaria. Not only that, but it's impossible in most places for them even to buy it. In the past, the Belgian government provided some medical care in Congo. They subsidized our four mission hospitals and dispensaries, providing the better share of the cost of running the hospitals and medical care. June 1960 changed this. A new government took over but it did not make any real provision for medical care, especially not at mission hospitals. To illustrate this point: at our hospital at Wasolo—prior to 1960 we received approximately $500 a month for salaries and general maintenance plus the bulk of medicine. The number of beds at that time was only 25. Now, the number was more than 80, and we received only $20 a month.

One day Phil walked into the house carrying a baby monkey that he had just bought from some of the village children. The monkey had to be bottle fed, and Phil found that a formula of milk and mashed bananas worked very well. It fell to Lyn and me to feed the monkey during the times that Phil was at the hospital. The monkey quickly became just like a spoiled child. It did not want to be enclosed in its box that Phil kept it in during the night, and one morning, as I went out to the kitchen to see about breakfast preparations, I observed that Phil had been sleeping on the living room couch.

"Why are you sleeping on that uncomfortable thing?" I asked.

"Well," Phil replied, "the monkey was so fretful during the night that I decided I would get out of the room."

"That's just the limit when you have to give up your room to a little monkey!" I remarked.

Phil celebrated his twenty-fifth birthday during his stay with us. Paul always wanted to make the most of birthdays, holidays, and anniversaries, and now that Phil was a member of our family, his birthday was no exception. To celebrate the occasion, we planned a surprise party for Phil, and invited some English-speaking friends of ours from the nearby trading village of Yakoma, the Cornelissens. "Cor," as we called him, had come originally from Holland, and was in charge of the cotton company in Yakoma. His wife, Muriel, was English. They often visited us, and we enjoyed the chance to talk with people who spoke English. We did manage to surprise Phil, and the evening was a jolly affair.

Only a few days after this happy occasion, we found ourselves suddenly faced with an emergency. Our own dear Flossie became seriously ill. She was treated for malaria, but soon after this first treatment, her twelve-year-old brother Matthieu came running up to our house crying, "Is the doctor here?"

"No, Matthieu, he's still at the hospital. What's the matter?"

"Flossie is trembling. She's so sick!"

"Run to the hospital quickly!" I left to Azupka the preparations for the noon meal that I was then making, and while Matthieu sprinted down Mango Lane to the hospital, I rushed to Flossie's house, but she was not there. I kept going, to the hospital, where several friends had already taken her. Paul was bending over her.

"I'm going to die," she whispered. "Something is choking me."

Jody had run for some medication that Paul wanted to administer and I knelt beside Flossie. She was lying on a low cot in the corridor of the hospital, for the building at that time was overflowing with patients and there was no bed available. We decided to take her to the vacant room in Jody's duplex. By the next afternoon she was so much worse that we felt close to despair. She clung to Paul and did not want him to leave her bedside. He stayed with her a good part of the night, and when morning came she rallied a bit.

As the week passed, she was intermittently worse and better, and while Paul and Jody took care of things at the hospital, I nursed Flossie. To make matters worse, that week Flossie's father was not in Wasolo but was attending church meetings at Karawa. Because transportation was so difficult, it was not possible to get him back to Wasolo ahead of schedule. We kept waiting for him to come, and finally on Friday afternoon, on the fifth day of Flossie's illness, he arrived. We were all overjoyed to see him. On Saturday, Flossie began having convulsions at noon. Paul's immediate worry was that she might have tetanus, too, as we had two tetanus cases at the hospital. We were beside ourselves and we prayed anxiously: "O Lord, what do we do? We so need Flossie here. She is such a help in the work, such a witness to the other girls. Help us to know what to do, how to care for her."

This was the weekend we were to leave for vacation. Paul had made arrangements for a short-term doctor at Karawa, Dr. Bob Etherington, to come to Wasolo for the two-week period that we would be away. Dr. Bob was due this same Saturday evening, and with him would be one of the Karawa nurses, Elsie Carlson, who had spent Christmas with us, and also our son, Wayne, who would join us for vacation because school was out. We planned to go to a lake in Ubangi Province where our missionaries vacation, but now we could not leave because Flossie's life hung in the balance.

At 6 p.m., Dr. Bob, Elsie, and Wayne arrived. We were relieved to see them and joyous to have our son back with us. Paul was especially glad to have someone on his professional level to help him. One of the things he missed most was getting together with other doctors to exchange information and review diagnoses. Here in the bush the decisions were primarily on his shoulders, and that evening Flossie's illness was a heavy burden on us all, particular because it could not be diagnosed with certainty. We took turns at her bedside.

After my turn, as evening drew near, a storm suddenly gathered. On Wasolo hill, an electrical storm was a beautiful sight, and as Dr. Bob and I headed to get a demijohn of water in the cookhouse, we could look across the valley and see fingers of lightning dissecting the evening sky in all directions. Paul, Phil, and the children were gathered in our house, and in the duplex, Jody and Elsie were staying with Flossie.

Dr. Bob marveled at how beautiful it was on the hill. "Yes it is," I said, "but I just don't like lightning."

An instant later, while we were in the cookhouse adjacent to the kitchen, a tremendous crash came, like an overpowering explosion, and everything seemed to flash orange. Immediately I thought the motor house had been hit, but when the rumble of the thunder had rolled away, I could still hear the regular rhythm of the motor. I shouted into the house to Paul, "Are you all right?" The house was in total darkness.

"Yes, we're all right."

A moment later, Jody and Elsie came running out. They had been praying at Flossie's bedside when suddenly they had heard the great explosion and some of their lights had gone out. They saw our house completely dark.

Dr. Bob turned to me, saying, "Now I share your healthy respect for electrical storms!"

Not until the next morning, Sunday, did we discover that lightning had struck a tree just a few feet from our cookhouse, knocking out fuses in our home. On Sunday Flossie took a decided turn for the better. Now we could breathe more easily, as she improved steadily, although we never knew really what her illness had been.

On Sundays we had no regular call-in of stations, but a noon listening time for radio so that messages could be given, and only those stations concerned would come in. After we returned to the house from church, we turned on the radio for the listening time. Our hearts were lighter because Flossie was so much better and we felt now that we would be able to get away on our vacation after all. On the radio we heard this message:

Nine-Q-Three-Two calling Nine-Q-Three-One and Nine-Q-Three-Nine, we have a message. Will you come in please? . . . Over.

What could Karawa be calling us about? Paul ran out to crank the motor for power to go on the air. As I heard the thump of the motor, I switched on the transmitter. It took a moment to warm up. The station calling us realized that it would take us a few moments, and it would wait five minutes before giving the call again.

We were on the air.

Nine-Q-Three-Nine to Nine-Q-Three-Two, we read you, Ann. Give us the message.

Three-Two to Three-Nine. We thought you would like to know that you will have guests this evening. A photographer, sent out by the drug company sponsoring Phil Littleford arrived here yesterday afternoon. His name is Priya Ramrakha. He's from Kenya. He has already left for Wasolo with a Congolese chauffeur, and Mark is going along too, to act as interpreter for him. They left at ten this morning. . . . Over.

To Three-One, they would like to have Kurt go along as company for Mark. . . . Over.

This news was a surprise to us. Smith, Kline & French had written asking Paul's permission to send a photographer to do a story on Phil Littleford for the *Baltimore Sunday Sun*. Paul had given his permission, but had asked them to wait until sometime in July, because the middle of June was to be our vacation period. Mark was Mark Enos, teenage son of one of our missionaries, and Kurt was our cousin, Kurt Lindquist, Margaret and Frank's son.

Paul responded to the message:

Nine-Q-Three-Nine to Nine-Q-Three-Two.... Yes, we certainly are interested in that message. That will change some plans, but we will be waiting for them tonight. You'll be glad to know that Flossie is improved today. She gave us a real scare yesterday. Dr. Bob and Elsie arrived safely last evening.... Over.

Nine-Q-Three-One to Nine-Q-Three-Two, we read your request concerning Kurt. We'll send him along.... Over and out.

I had little time to prepare for our latest arrivals. Everything seemed to be in chaos at our station. At that moment Jody came into our living room, and I said to her, "Do you remember what you said to me the first time we met?"

Jody just grinned. It was in 1961, when Paul was on his way to Congo for the first time, that I had met Jody. She was finishing a furlough, about to start back for Congo, and was visiting one day in my home church in Menominee, Michigan, where the children and I were staying while Paul was away. The church in Menominee had part of her missionary support. When I learned that Jody was stationed in Congo, I told her that Paul was on his way there but had no idea where he would be assigned. She quickly said, "Well, there's no chance of his getting to Wasolo where I am to be stationed. It's way up at the end of the world. No one ever comes to Wasolo."

Priya Ramrakha was a *Time-Life* photographer, and was loaned to Smith, Kline & French for this assignment. He spent three days taking pictures of all phases of the work at our station. Phil was in the foreground, of course, but many of the pictures included Paul also. Priya took pictures in the wards, at the dispensary, outside the hospital, inside the hospital, the operating room, the leper colony. He experienced a pirogue ride, too, when the doctors crossed the river to give polio shots in a neighboring village—three busy days. During this time, we were nursing Flossie back to health, also.

By Thursday the picture-taking was finished, Flossie was much better, the hospital was left in the hands of Dr. Bob, and we were off on vacation at last.

Priya went with us as far as Karawa. When we parted he assured us he had had a marvelous time, but he added that he was going to request not to be sent on assignment to Congo again. Originally the assignment had been planned for five days—three days to be spent at Wasolo taking pictures, one day travel time in either direction. Actually, the assignment had taken Priya thirteen days, and of those thirteen, only three had been spent photographing at Wasolo. He, too, had found that Wasolo was way up at the end of the world.

There was a lovely lake—Kwada—not far from the station at Karawa, which had been set aside as a vacation and rest spot for missionaries. At the lakeside were four small cottages so that several families could be there at one time. The water was clear and fresh, the lake being fed by underground springs. It was a lovely spot, a place to get away from the pressures of the hospital. Paul was badly in need of rest. Because Dr. Bob was at Wasolo, Paul felt at ease about taking his vacation, and he relaxed completely. Wayne and Lyn had a perfect time, and Lyn learned to swim within the first three days at the lake. But all vacations come to an end, and so did ours, on June 30, which was Independence Day for Congo. On this particular date—June 30, 1964—the United Nations troops would be pulling out. Also, there was a change in government that day. Prime Minister Cyrille Adoula resigned and Moise Tshombé, who had been head of the rebellious Katanga Province, now became prime minister of Congo. Independence Day was to be marked with a big three-day celebration, and we decided that we should not be on the road during those days. So we stayed at Kwada a little longer. There was some apprehension that soldiers at the road-blocks—established for routine questioning of all travelers during those days of political unrest—might be drunk because of the celebrations and that there might be other difficulties in traveling. As it turned out, things were very quiet in our area.

We went back to our duties at Wasolo, and Dr. Bob and Elsie returned to Karawa. With us on our return to Wasolo from Karawa were Bob and Janet Thornbloom. Bob, our missionary mechanic, was going to try to repair the motor at the hospital light plant so that Paul could have lights in the hospital operating room and electricity for the portable x-ray machine that had been shipped to Wasolo hospital several months before our arrival.

Setting up the x-ray machine was one of the first projects Paul dived into almost as soon as we arrived. He was not mechanically inclined, but he followed the directions carefully and got the unit set up. However, when he went to turn on the electric motor, he discovered that the voltage regulator was not working properly, so the x-ray unit would not function. He was as disappointed as a young boy who has set up an electric train only to find out that it will not run. With the light plant repaired, Paul would have use of this valuable equipment. Also, Bob had high hopes of being able to lay piping and repair the motor for the well, so that when the next dry season came we could have water from that. However, the well gave Bob no end of trouble, and he was not able to make the necessary repairs.

The Thornblooms stayed with us for two weeks then returned to Karawa. Phil went also to spend several weeks working at the Karawa hospital. By then, the third week in July, it was time for Congolese Girls' Bible Camp, near the Tandala station. Jody was to go and Flossie had recovered sufficiently so that she could go, too, along with several other girls from our area.

As the sound of the truck faded in the distance, all was quiet. Only our family remained atop the hill at Wasolo. Even Azupka and his family were no longer there. The missionary who had "loaned" Azupka to us was returning from furlough, and he had returned to Gbado. After these hectic weeks we enjoyed being alone for a few days. Never again would anyone be able to persuade me that no one ever comes to Wasolo.

VIII

Threatening Days—and a Wedding

The general excitement surrounding the departure of Flossie and the other girls for Bible camp was heightened by a radio message we received from Art Lundblad at Gemena during regular radio contact time.

Nine-Q-Three-Three to Three-Nine. . . . I had a letter today from Leola and she says that Paul Sedua may arrive in Congo soon. He has applied for his visa, so you may be having a wedding up your way. . . . Over.

Paul Sedua! He was a young Congolese now studying in Brussels, and we knew that he and Flossie had been corresponding for some time—as frequently as our infrequent mail service allowed. They were both of the Ngbaka tribe, came from neighboring villages, and had known each other from earlier years. Paul had been educated in our mission schools and then sent to Brussels for further study. He had been gone about three years. Within the last two years, he and Flossie had renewed their acquaintance, by letters and exchange of pictures. There had been occasional rumors that Flossie might be sent to Brussels and that they would be married, but they were only rumors, and Art's message came as a great surprise to me. The usual hum of the transmitter filled the room as I waited, rather impatiently, for Wasolo's turn to respond. When my turn came, I said excitedly:

Nine-Q-Three-Nine to Three-Three.... Read your message, Art... we must find out more about this.... Why, even Flossie doesn't know.... Please give us more details after regular transmission.... Over.

I waited through the usual call-ins, the squeaks, the hums, the buzzes, the chit-chat of the radio stations, until Gemena's turn came again.

Nine-Q-Three-Three to Three-Nine.... Don't get excited.... It isn't definite.... I'll talk with you after regular transmission.... Over.

Don't get excited! It was past mid-July, and I knew school would start in September in Brussels, so the wedding, if it was to take place, would have to be within a few weeks. Flossie would have to have dresses made not only for the wedding but to go on to Brussels. I knew she had nothing suitable for such a different place, and I knew that most of the work would fall to Jody and me to get material. My barrel of sewing supplies—would I have anything suitable? I was almost overwhelmed with the thought of the hundreds of things we would have to do in such a short time.

The after-transmission produced nothing more definite. Paul Sedua in a letter to missionary Leola Johnson, then in Leopoldville, had mentioned the possibility that he would be coming back to Congo, assuming, of course, that we already knew. However, mail service had been poor in our area for many months, and his latest letters to Flossie had not arrived. The "Bumba Express" made only a few runs after our arrival in Congo, and then gave out completely because of inadequate care and almost impassable roads. Our mail reached Bumba by air, but then had to come the last 160 miles by truck. We had been depending on the Yakoma *commerçants*—the Portuguese merchants—to bring the mail when they had errands in Bumba. So occasionally we had mail delivery once a week, sometimes once in a month or six weeks, and sometimes none at all. As we found later, Paul Sedua had realized the inadequacy of our mail service, and so had written to Leola also, assuming that she would relay the message in case Flossie had not received his letters.

As soon as after-transmission was through, I rushed out to give Flossie the message. It was a pleasant, indeed an overwhelming, surprise for her. Then I told Paul and Jody. What excitement around our house! But Flossie preferred not to tell anyone else except her family until plans became more definite. Although Flossie was surprised to learn that Paul Sedua was on his way then, I'm not sure that she was completely surprised at the turn of events. Occasionally we would tease her about her letters to and from Brussels but she would only smile and turn away.

Amidst this air of pleasant suspense, Flossie departed for Girls' Bible Camp near Tandala.

Late in the afternoon following the girls' departure, just as everything seemed to have calmed down temporarily, another emergency arose to shatter the peace of the day. A Catholic *père* (father) came riding, huffing and puffing on his bicycle. That in itself was unusual, because the Catholic fathers usually came by truck, but we learned from this father that the bridge at Targini was again washed out and he had had to leave his truck and borrow a bicycle in order to get to Paul. Another priest at the Catholic mission in Yakoma was very ill and had been vomiting blood. Of course this called for immediate action, and Paul rushed off at once with the priest.

Paul found the *père* very low—so low, in fact, that he didn't want to come to Wasolo for treatment, but preferred to remain at the Yakoma mission and, as he said, "just die." Paul remained with him several hours, giving emergency treatment, and then as the priest seemed to be out of immediate danger he returned to Wasolo.

The next day the Cornelissens drove up to our house in their truck to tell Paul that the *père* was very low again—and would he come right away? Paul felt that by this time the *père* had lost so much blood that it would require a transfusion, which would not be the easiest thing to accomplish under the circumstances. He returned to Yakoma with the Cornelissens. Fortunately, we had some blood-typing serum, and Paul sent out a plea to the *commerçants* and to the priests to come in and have their blood tested, to see which one could give his blood to the desperately ill *père*. It seemed that all the *commerçants* in the area were suddenly very busy and unavailable! However, it was found that Père Leopold's blood was compatible with the older *père's*.

Paul had come to know Père Leopold the best of any of the priests in Yakoma because Père Leopold rode a motorcycle and occasionally came to

Wasolo for a visit. On one occasion he had dinner with us. With the transfusion the strength of the older *père* returned, and with further medication and nursing care by one of the sisters, and by Muriel Cornelissen who was a nurse, he grew much better. Paul warned the *père* that as soon as his strength was to the point where he could travel, he should return to his home in Belgium. Should trouble come in Congo, Paul explained, he would not have the strength or the stamina to endure the hardships that might ensue. By now, we had been hearing disquieting reports of rebel turmoil in Stanleyville, to the south of us. We did not know whether it would spread, but the thought of possible trouble in the future was on our minds. However, we did not believe that the trouble would spread to Wasolo, which was so far away, so difficult of access, and not on the road to any place the rebels might want.

Meanwhile, things were bustling at Wasolo. Carl "Cully" Edstrom, our missionary builder, who built many of the mission structures in the Ubangi, including the house we were living in, and his wife, Vivian, had come from Bumba to do some urgent repair work on Jody's duplex. As Paul said, "The termites are doing a better job of eating Jody's house than she is of living in it." We could actually see the walls and the ceilings disintegrate. Jody claimed that at night she could hear the termites crunching. Cully attempted to remake several walls from cement blocks, which the termites could not eat.

The days were filled with masons and carpenters banging and making noise, along with the other activities that always went on at Wasolo—the comings and goings of patients, the ringing of the church bell for services, the jabber and excitement of the children, the sounds of people working, the preparation of meals and the washing of clothes, praying and ministering, the beating of a drum somewhere.

While the Edstroms were with us, time came for the Wasolo Regional Church Conference. Paul had been asked to give a message at the Sunday afternoon service, to be held at a village several kilometers away. It had been raining very hard, and the road was bad, but Paul and Cully hopped on their bicycles to ride to the village where the service was being held.

Paul's message that day was in simple language, for he still could not speak Lingala eloquently. But the message had a real and vital warning for the people, and in it he took note of the increasing political strife in Congo. Paul said:

Greetings to all of you. I am happy to see you all. At a big conference like this, there is much joy. It is a joy to hear about the work of the Church. It is a joy to see everyone.

At this conference, we are going to think about following Jesus. It is not hard to follow Jesus when all goes well, but sometimes it is difficult to follow him when the road is difficult.

Since your last meeting in 1963, much has happened to the Church in Congo. I feel that God would have us think about some of the things I have heard and read about the Church in Congo in 1964.

When I went to Leopoldville, I saw Mlle. Verna Lundgren* and many other missionaries and Congolese Christians who had to leave Kwilu.

Why?

A man named Mulele Pierre went to Egypt, and then to China. The Chinese taught him to hate Christians and they taught him how to wage war and help Antoine Gizenga overtake the government of Congo. He returned in 1963 to begin doing just what others did long ago in China. I think you all know that missionaries went to China a long time ago. Our missionaries worked there for Jesus, but when the Communists took over the government they sent away all the missionaries. This happened seventeen years ago. They killed one of our doctors and two of our women missionaries. They killed many Christians. Nearly all of the true Christians who followed Jesus were killed.

M. Mulele Pierre went to Kwilu and there he organized La Jeunesse. He taught them how to fight as others had done in China many years ago. Today I will tell you only about one mission. The name of the mission is Kandala in Kwilu Province.

Before the 15th of January, the people of the mission heard that La Jeunesse had started to destroy many places. There was great fear! On the night of the fifteenth, La Jeunesse beat many people and they killed

---

*Verna Lundgren had been a missionary at Wasolo several years before this time.

the Chef du Secteur. They burned his house—the 17th of January, La Jeunesse destroyed the ferry at the river. The 20th, the secteur was burned. The 21st, there was fighting at Kandala. During the day, everyone walked about with great fear. Many ran into the forest with their possessions. Night came. They heard much noise. They looked! What is this? They saw La Jeunesse burn the village. They burned the school. They burned the Bible school and all the student houses and all their belongings. They burned the houses of the missionaries and of the pastors. They burned all the trucks. Nearly the whole mission was burned. They captured the missionaries and kept them in one place, and they captured the pastors and kept them in another place. They took their glasses, their shoes, their watches; they took their money. They destroyed everything.

What remained?

The word of God! God says: "I will watch over you," and in Psalm 23, we will say with David: "Though I walk through the valley of the shadow of death, I will fear no evil."

They spoke unkindly to the Christians. It was still night. People prayed. They did not know if some had already been killed. They did not know whether they would die in the morning, or not. They could not sleep. The sun came up. They set them free. They rejoiced, for no one had died. But they were sad because the whole mission was destroyed—all in one night. How did it all end? They made the missionaries leave. The pastor took the students from the Bible school into the forest. They walked until they came to another province. The students went all the way to Leo [Leopoldville] where they could meet with their professors, and to finish their studies.

But it did not end this way in every place. In Leo, I talked to a Protestant missionary doctor who came out of another part of Kwilu. He said that the people of the Catholic mission sent for him and another missionary to come and help bury three Belgian priests and one *abbé* [abbot]. They forced the sisters to leave.

Today in Congo, the Christians of Kwilu, of Bukavu, of Katanga, and I heard yesterday, of Kivu, are suffering for Jesus. And what they did in Kwilu, they are trying to do in Coq [Coquilhatville], in Stan [Stanleyville]. And now in Yakoma and Gemena—many soldiers have been sent to guard the roads in order to protect the province from these evil men.

We do not know what will happen in 1964—and in 1965—until we meet together again. We do not know if we will have to suffer or die during this year because we are Christians. But it does not matter! Our job is to follow Jesus. Joseph [Gebanga Joseph] will read 1 Peter 2:21-24. Yes, Jesus suffered much for us. Since he suffered so much in order to save us, shall we not be willing to suffer for him? Joseph will also read 1 Peter 4:12, 13, 16, and 19.

It wasn't only Jesus who suffered. Stephen was stoned. They beheaded James. Paul knew much suffering—we read in 2 Corinthians, chapter 11, that he was beaten often, he was put in prison in a deep cave, three times he was shipwrecked—and through it all he remained a Christian. He was not afraid, and he said in Philippians 1:29 that we are not only to believe in Christ, but also suffer for his sake.

For 300 years after Paul, Christians were burned, they were thrown to the lions, they were run over by trucks until they died. But the Church of Jesus Christ did not die because of it. Jesus said: "I will go with you."

How does all of this apply to us at Wasolo? Jesus is asking us if we are willing to suffer for him. This is of greatest importance to all of us Christians here today.

We are going to gather together at the Lord's Table. Before taking part, I think each one should ask himself if he is willing to suffer for Jesus Christ if need be—and if he is willing even to die if necessary—during this coming year. Taking part in Communion means union with Jesus. Union with Jesus sometimes means joy—but union with Jesus sometimes means suffering. My friends, if today you are not willing to suffer for Jesus, do not partake of the elements. If you do take the cup and the bread here today, be certain that you are willing to give your life for Jesus during 1964 or 1965 if it is necessary. To follow Jesus means to be willing to suffer for him.

Will you follow Jesus this year?

I will ask Pastor Bangi to lead us in prayer.

This message was given to the Congolese in our area less than two months before many of them would die, and shortly thereafter Paul, too, would stand the test of these words.

During this period, we heard over the station radio that Flossie, still at camp, had received a letter from Paul Sedua, that he would be at Wasolo within a short time, and that there would, indeed, be a wedding. How happy this news made us all! Now, looking back on it, I realize that the marriage plans were actually signaling the beginning of the end of our time at Wasolo.

Flossie arrived home from camp, and on August 6 we were told that Paul Sedua had arrived at Gemena and that he and Flossie would be married at Wasolo on August 22. Coming from three years in Europe, we knew that he would expect a Western-style church wedding. This meant a lot of preparation for us, because in Wasolo it was not easy to run out and get things that one needed for a wedding. That same evening—August 6—over the Voice of America broadcast came the dreadful news that Stanleyville had fallen to the rebels.

The next morning we heard on radio that a family and two men, who had been working with the Congo Polytechnic Institute at Gemena but were being transferred to Stanleyville University, had been on the riverboat to Stanleyville but had turned back. The following day we heard the full story of what had happened when the two men who had been on the boat stopped in Wasolo. They were on the regular riverboat, they told us, that goes down the Congo River to Stanleyville. When the boat came within a short distance of the city, another small boat came up to them and someone aboard shouted, "Don't go into Stan! Go back to Bumba! Stan has fallen." As they were turning around in mid-river, another boat came into view and rapidly gained on them. It was filled with National Congolese soldiers. They came alongside and, pouring onto the escaping boat, went back upriver to Bumba. It was night time when the boat finally pulled alongside the embankment at Bumba.

The Edstroms lived in Bumba and from their house, alongside the river, they heard the commotion, heard a knocking at their door, and became frightened. Cautiously they opened the door to find the people from the boat standing there, very excited, trying to explain what had happened. The ANC (Armée National Congolaise) soldiers took up residence in the building next door to the Edstroms' home. The incident naturally caused the rest of us missionaries much uneasiness and uncertainty. The two men who told us the story stayed with us for the weekend and then went on their way to the adjoining country, the Central African Republic.

Stanleyville was still a long way from Wasolo, a long way from the Ubangi. Yet we knew that the rebel forces could proceed up the river to Bumba. We began to feel that our days at Wasolo might be numbered. Time might be running out for us in our work with these people whom we had come to know and love.

That Sunday evening Chaplain Vuku, Wanzi, and his brother Joseph came to our house to talk and have a time of prayer. They said they didn't want any of us to endanger our lives and that if we felt we must go, they would understand. Paul assured them that we would take every precaution, but that we would not leave until we felt it was absolutely necessary.

Our days continued to be very busy. Flossie had returned from camp, of course, but Jody had gone to Lake Kwada for her vacation. Flossie and I busily began to make preparations for her coming wedding. Also, there were many things she wanted to learn. She wanted to know how to cook on a gas stove, how to prepare some of the meals that she would be expected to know about in Brussels. She knew how to sew, but now she was eager to become more expert. She had always spent a good deal of time with Jody and us in our homes, so she was familiar with many Western ways of life; how useful that would be to her now! We were happy for her forthcoming marriage, and yet we knew we would sorely miss her friendship, as well as her work with the maternity patients at the hospital.

Flossie wanted Lynette and her own little sister Marie, who was about Lyn's age, to be candle lighters. I rummaged in the barrel where I kept my sewing supplies and found some material that would be appropriate to make dresses for the girls. Fortunately, Paul Sedua had a wedding dress for Flossie which he had purchased in Brussels.

We set to work altering skirts and a dress that missionaries had given to Flossie for the cold Brussels winter, and making other garments she would need. The days slipped by in a round of preparations mixed with mounting doubts as to how long we would able to stay at Wasolo. The news of the political situation continued to be discouraging. Rebel troops were active to the southeast, and seemed to be causing more trouble with each passing day. Now, of course, there was no United Nations force to keep order, and only the ANC, the National Congolese army, to defend the country against the marauding Jeunesse and Simbas, or lion-men, as the rebels called themselves.

Tuesday, August 18. We did not hear the Bumba transmitter. This did not alarm us too much as there were often power failures, and yet there was uneasiness because we knew danger could be lurking along the river. Still, we told ourselves, Bumba's antenna was beamed to the west, Gemena, and toward Karawa. We often had difficulty making contact with them. But on this day no one else had heard Bumba, either.

Wednesday, August 19. Nothing from Bumba. No hum of transmitter. Nothing. Also, we knew that Jody and Paul Sedua had left the day before from Karawa for the journey to Wasolo. They had not yet arrived. We did not know what to do at radio time that day. There were plans to send a truck from Karawa and another from Wasolo (because nobody was at the intermediate point, Gbado, this particular day) to look for them. Just as we were about to sign off on radio, a note arrived by a courier on bicycle. It was from Jody, saying that they were stuck in the mud at Nzale with a broken tie rod. We breathed a sigh of relief. At least it was only the normal trouble and delay.

We knew they were within two hours of Wasolo. Quickly we relayed the message to Karawa:

Three-Nine to Three-Two. . . . Received word from Jody; they are stuck at Nzale. Everything O.K. . . . everything O.K. We have chauffeur to go. Did you read me? Everything O.K. with Jody. . . . Did you read me? Over.

Roger, Three-Nine! Good. Good to hear that. . . . Off and over.

Fortunately there was a truck and a driver on hand who could go out and help, and he brought Paul Sedua and Jody back to the station within a short time.

Thursday, August 20. Two days before the wedding and still an immense amount of work to do. The rain had started. Paul and Jody were unpacking some medicines from the Christian Medical Society that had been a year and a half getting to Congo. Suddenly a truck drove up to the station, and a Greek *commerçant* bolted out and ran to our house. "Bumba has fallen!" he shouted. "You must leave!"

At that time our mission truck and the chauffeur were about fifty kilometers away, at Wapinda, on an errand. But our fears were not for ourselves, they were for the Edstroms at Bumba where the danger was so close. This was the third day that we had not heard their transmitter, and now, at 3 p.m., we had received fearful news. At four o'clock there was to be a regular call-in time; it was still rainy and stormy, very poor weather for transmission. Paul went out to turn on the motor, warmed up the transmitter, flipped the switch, and called the familiar words:

Nine-Q-Three-Nine, this is Nine-Q-Three-Nine to Nine-Q-Three-Zero, come in please... come in please, Three-Zero. Three-Zero from Three-Nine, come in please.... Over.

The switch was thrown and we listened. Nothing. He repeated it over and over. We knew that there was small chance of anyone hearing us, but then suddenly the hum of another transmitter came piercing through the usual confusion of blank sounds that were vying on the airwaves.

This is Nine-Q-Three-Seven. We read you, Three-Nine, go ahead.... Over. ... Three-Nine to Three-Seven... A crash of thunder came roaring over us. *... Bad news concerning Three-Zero.... Where are Cully and Viv?... Where are the Edstroms?... Over.*

An oscillating whine followed and then the steady *da-dit-da-dit-dit-dit-dit* of a telegraph key from some unknown corner of the Ubangi came chirping over the loudspeaker. From this criss-cross of sound we heard a voice fading in:

... Get out! Get out of there, Three-Nine... out! Another thunderous crash from the loudspeaker. *Three-Nine, do you read us? Over.*

Another crash of thunder enveloped us, close to our hill now. This was no time for transmission! Paul hunched forward, holding the microphone closer: *Not us...not Three-Nine...Three-Zero, Three Zero...Edstroms...Edstroms...Where are the Edstroms?...Over.*

The chirping sound of another transmitter came then, and the background of static and jabbering signals receded a bit. *This is Three-Two, this is Three-Two...Viv and Cully just drove in....Edstroms just arrived....Over.*

Tears of joy welled in our eyes. The Edstroms were safe in Karawa. Outside the storm continued, as did the storm in our minds and our hearts.

Danger was getting closer now. The rebels seemed to be following the Congo River. We knew precautions had to be taken, that we must be alert to any rumor that might come our way. We finally went to bed with heavy hearts, not knowing what the morrow would bring.

Friday, August 21. The day before the wedding. The weather, at least, had improved. We received word that the church truck with Pastor Zacharie Alengi (Pastor Doko's successor as president of the Ubangi Church and the minister who was to perform the ceremony) had left the Karawa station and was headed up to Wasolo. We did want this wedding to take place if at all possible, and we clung to that hope in our thoughts and plans.

Saturday, August 22. The wedding day. Paul went into Yakoma to get flowers from the Catholic mission for the wedding, as none were in bloom on our station just then. The sisters had graciously consented to his request for some. He was excited and happy about the wedding and wanted it to be as beautiful as possible. As Paul approached town he saw people rushing out—women with belongings on their heads, old people walking away rapidly from their village. Yakoma itself, he found, was practically deserted, like a tomb. The ANC soldiers were leaving. They said that they had been called to Gemena. Their departure stirred up the villagers, who also decided to leave.

Paul returned to Wasolo and we had our regular two o'clock contact with our other stations. It was decided that we should pack and go. The wedding was scheduled for four o'clock. At the time this news came, I was trimming the wedding cake, and I was so upset that many unplanned-for squiggles and curlicues got into the frosting by mistake.

111

What should we do, we wondered. The rain started. It poured! There was our answer: nothing moved when the rain came, and we decided that the thing to do was to proceed with the wedding.

Just a few minutes before the ceremony the rain eased. Paul drove the bridal party down to the church so that they would not get wet. Lyn and Marie lit the candles and Paul Sedua and Florence Bangi were married in a lovely Christian ceremony, performed by Pastor Alengi and assisted by her father, Pastor Bangi.

There were very few Christian church weddings in our area. Flossie's father was radiating happiness that the ceremony took place in the Wasolo church. He felt it would be a good example to the young people in the area. The bride and groom made a joyous couple, obviously as happy as could be.

Then the party moved back up the hill to our house, where the reception was to be held. We had asked the Bangi family if we might give the reception as our token of love to the couple. This offer was heartily accepted! We had originally planned to string some lights in the yard, because by this time it was dark. The rain changed that plan, however, and instead we had the reception for about sixty people inside our house. Somehow we managed to get enough tables together. We used sheets for tablecloths, and for a wedding feast there was a combination of goat and pig with gravy sauce, poured over bowls of steaming rice. There were peas, rolls, and then wedding cake and coffee with lots of sugar and milk. Gay as the evening was, we all felt a dark cloud hovering over us. This might be the last bit of merriment for a long time.

Immediately after the reception everyone's thoughts turned more serious. Guests who had come from Karawa wondered if they should leave immediately. The feeling was that if trouble should come, people would be safer in their own tribal areas. Paul discussed this with them. The roads were bad because of the heavy rain, and it was decided that it would be best for everyone to get a night's sleep before starting home. It was then that Jody said wearily, "Certainly nothing more can happen!"

Jody had turned her house over as a guest house and was planning to spend the night with us. She went across to the duplex to see that all the guests had places to sleep and enough blankets. When she got there, she found the brother of the groom feeling ill. She called Paul over, and it was soon discovered that the unfortunate man had a strangulated hernia. The case was not yet severe, and Paul decided that it would not be well to operate and then send the man on the truck the next morning to his own tribal area. The best thing was to have him rest and to give him hypos, which Flossie could administer, until he could get back to Dr. Helen at Karawa, where he could undergo surgery.

Flossie and Paul Sedua were packing by then, as they had decided to leave the next morning also. By this time my nerves and emotions had caught up with me. The sight of Flossie packing, when she had originally planned to spend several days at Wasolo before going on her wedding trip, brought the gravity of the situation home to me. I broke down and said that if we were ordered to leave, I hoped the order would state that all had to leave, because I knew that Paul would want to stay as long as he could to help the people at Wasolo.

After assisting Flossie in her packing, I had to gather the things together that Phil Littleford had left at our house during his stay in Karawa. He would not be returning, owing to the serious news, so his things would have to be sent to him in the truck the following morning. My next job was to pack emergency bags for ourselves, in case we had to leave at a moment's notice. We had no plans for leaving during that night. The rain had been coming down steadily, and we knew that the roads were all but impassable, especially in the dark. The only thing to do was to wait until morning, and see what developed.

Early the next morning, Sunday, August 23, we had to bid our guests and our new bridal couple goodbye. I saw tears in Paul's eyes as he said goodbye to Flossie. He loved her dearly and would miss her in the work. He realized that the new life she was facing would at times be very difficult for her, very different from the life she was used to in the "bush." Little did he realize at this time what all of us would be facing within a few days.

This was no time for emotions to overtake us, however. There was so much to be done. The house needed some attention after the reception. We might have to leave within a short time and much had to be taken care of. Rice and bits of food were scattered over the floor. We counted eighteen sheets that we had used for tablecloths. The small babies would always come with their mothers and they did not wear plastic pants, so there were puddles here and there. We had asked the cooks working for us then if they would please work for us on Sunday, which ordinarily they did not do. We told them a little about the urgency of events, and they agreed to help us. We took time off only for the morning service. Fortunately the sun was shining so the clothes were drying, and we continued to pack. We did not know whether we would be in the house one hour, one day, or for how long. We prayed that the Lord would give us presence of mind and peace.

We did stay—that day. We sent a Congolese carpenter, who had relatives in Kemba, the African village across the river from Yakoma, in the Central African Republic, to see if an unoccupied house Jody knew of there would be available for our use in the event that we had to leave Wasolo quickly. He did not return by nightfall, so we dropped into bed, not knowing exactly what was happening. However, we did plan to leave the next morning, Monday. We awakened to a drenching rain.

"It's as if God had sent the floods to give us time to breathe," said Paul. We could not leave.

IX

The River between Us

The heavy downpour of Monday, August 24, provided another respite, and we continued packing. Late that afternoon our carpenter, who had gone across the Ubangi River to Kemba to inquire about a house for us to use there, returned to Wasolo. There was an old Baptist Mid-Missions missionary home located there. The African pastor, our carpenter reported, said that we would be welcome to come over whenever we needed to. They would be waiting for us.

On Tuesday morning, a radio report indicated that things were somewhat better. We decided to wait again. That would give us another day, perhaps, or at least a few hours.

Paul took the truck into Yakoma to size up the situation there. He found that the contingent of ANC soldiers had returned and things seemed fairly calm. Late that evening, a mission employee came running to us excitedly saying that according to a report, two or three rebels had come to Monga, across the Uele and Bili rivers from Yakoma, had killed some inhabitants, and threatened to come to Yakoma the next day. There was no barge or bridge, no means whatever for taking vehicles across, but Paul felt that he should go again into Yakoma and ask the soldiers about this new crisis.

The soldiers assured him that they would keep careful guard over the river to see that no one came across by canoe without authorization. We decided that we should leave the area Wednesday morning. Again on Wednesday, however, came the torrential rains. Again we could not go anywhere and we knew that no one could come to us.

By the end of the week the general news reports from all over the area were much more encouraging. In fact, by Monday, August 31, there was a school board meeting via radio to discuss the possibility of opening the new school session of Ubangi Academy the following week. We did not feel comfortable about the prospect of sending the children to the Karawa station, though. This would be Lyn's first year there, and Wayne's second, so we would have no child at home.

From all reports, the movement of the rebel forces was going downriver; what they wanted were the provincial capitals, which in the Ubangi was Gemena. If they followed the roads, they would have to go through Karawa to reach Gemena. Suddenly, while the radio meeting of the school board was in progress, one of our other stations interrupted with the message:

To all stations! We just heard that Lisala has been taken! Lisala! Word from the embassy is that we should evacuate at least women and children!

This immediately changed any plans for starting school at Karawa, because we knew then that troops were moving in the direction we feared, and that they could easily come to the area where we would be sending the children. Now all of us fell to talking by means of the radio, wondering just how long we could stay at each station. We heard right then that reinforcements of soldiers were arriving in Gemena. So the day of August 31, which had begun so calmly with thoughts of reopening school, ended with anxious questioning and wondering: Who might be leaving? Who would risk staying? Where? What? How?

The next two days saw a lot of movement at our other mission stations. We, meanwhile, continued packing, and were ready to leave at almost a moment's notice. Each time that we thought we were ready to go, however, something came up that forced us to stay—an operation, an emergency obstetrical case, or the rain. During these few days five of the patients would certainly have died had Paul not been there. Three were expectant mothers, so the number was actually more than five as neither mothers nor babies would have survived.

The morning of September 3, again a rainy day, found us still at Wasolo, and we heard that our stations at Karawa, Gemena, Goyongo, and Bokada were also still staffed. The rain continued into the early hours of Friday, September 4, but skies were clearing by the time we arose and we knew that now we must obey the order that women and children leave as soon as possible. We had hoped against hope that we wouldn't have to leave. However, the wearing uncertainty from hour to hour as to what might happen was beginning to tell on us. The children, Jody, and I knew we must go.

It was a tearful and sad leave-taking from Wasolo that morning in the truck. We left for Yakoma, hoping in our hearts that this was only a warning and that soon we might be back. But there was no assurance in our hearts, no feeling of confidence as to what might happen. We had discussed and prayed with our station leaders, and Paul and I had talked things over and prayed. It was decided that Paul should take us across the Ubangi River into Central African Republic and then return to the station and take care of those who needed him so desperately in this vast area that was otherwise without a doctor.

Just as I had never asked Paul to stay away from a patient who needed him when he was in practice in the United States, I never begged him to stay away from a patient when we were in Congo. We both knew he was needed. We knew he must stay as long as he felt safe to do so.

We took the truck to the river's edge in Yakoma, went through customs formalities, packed our things into a pirogue, and crossed the river under a sunny sky. About mid-river we began to think we were a little foolish to leave. Things were so calm, so peaceful. The pirogue looked strange with camp stove, camp cots, suitcases, trunks, pots and pans crammed in. Somehow an air of lightness filled us, as if we were merely going on a picnic.

At last the other shore came floating up to us, the pirogue jarred quietly on the mud bottom, and the stern began to swing downstream under the current's pull. The rowers beached the boat and we were in the Central African

Republic. Again the usual customs formalities faced us and were quickly over. Then our good helpers gave us a hand to get our belongings up the long, sloping hill to the large mud-brick house with a grass roof in which, many years earlier, missionaries had lived. Not until we were on our way up the hill did we realize that it was not empty, as we had understood, but was occupied by the Kemba African pastor who had sent us the cordial message of welcome through our carpenter. He insisted upon moving out into an even older house so that we would have a place to stay. Paul, Jody, and I looked the house over and he made a mental note of the things we needed that he might bring over on his next trip. We got settled fairly comfortably, and then Paul, with some of our dear Congolese friends—Wanzi, Gebanga Joseph, and Vuku among them—was off again, back across the Ubangi River to Yakoma and then the few miles to Wasolo to resume work at the hospital. He planned to return to us on Sunday, and we eagerly looked forward to his visit.

Jody, the children, and I proceeded to set up housekeeping in our new surroundings. We had brought enough food, most of it canned, for a two-week stay. Then we discovered that we had forgotten a can opener. The African pastor found a rather rusty one among his possessions, which he gladly loaned to us. The first crisis in our new home was over.

Sunday dawned a lovely, sunny day. Almost from the first cock crow of sunrise we anticipated Paul's arrival. We went to the village church services and were welcomed warmly by the people there. After the service, there was even a parade and singing to welcome us to the village of Kemba.

Paul arrived much later than we expected. Emergency surgery had delayed him. He ate Sunday dinner with us and described the situation across the river. His plans were to go into Yakoma on Tuesday and get his pass papers, which he had to have. Jody and I had gotten ours about a week previously, but Paul purposely did not get his at the time we did because he felt it might be cause for alarm among the officials in town. Then he planned to come back to see us early Wednesday morning. He was thinking of staying with us after that.

We walked down to the river with him. It was beginning to rain somewhat, so he told us not to come all the way down to the water's edge. Wayne and Lyn took their turns clambering onto him, giving him a big kiss and hug. We were literally in the middle of the village, so ours was the quick kiss and parting typical of a morning when Paul was going off for the day's work. After all, it was a mere crossing of a wide river, and about a half-hour drive from Yakoma into the Wasolo station. He would not be far away at all, or long in returning.

We had no feeling of immediate danger that day. Paul had carefully laid plans for several escape routes from Wasolo if the necessity arose. On our side of the river we had a transistor radio at the house and with it we could listen to the transmissions from our stations still staffed in the Ubangi field. Paul told us he would come on a few minutes early each morning for a good-morning chat and to tell us how the patients were and how he was. So with a cheerful, "I'll see you on Wednesday morning," he and some of our Congolese friends who had come with him were off. Among them was Bomba Boniface, one of the nurses, who assured us, "We will take good care of Dr. Paul." They climbed into their pirogue, slipped away from shore, and moved across the river.

One of Paul's reasons for choosing Wednesday to come over was to be able to help some of our Congolese friends, who liked to cross over for the big market day on Wednesday mornings. We settled down and waited for Wednesday to come. Jody and I even started some lessons in the tribal language with a Mongbandi girl.

Monday was calm. We heard the regular transmissions between our mission stations, and the voices on the airwaves seemed unruffled, although obviously alert for possible threat to the security of any of the stations. We continued to get settled in our mud house. The rains at night proved that the roof was very leaky and we had to regroup our beds so we wouldn't get drenched. The drops became small torrents, and we listened to the rain on the sobi-grass roof. We relaxed somewhat after the weeks of being so very busy at Wasolo.

Tuesday morning we heard our remaining stations as usual. The day went on in ordinary fashion. We were anticipating Paul's visit the following day, and we looked forward to the goodies he had promised to have the cook bake for us. Also we were waiting somewhat impatiently for things that we had forgotten to bring over. It was a pleasant thought that Paul would be coming over to stay with us at a time when tension was high. We felt that we all could stand a relief from the tensions of recent days. Tuesday evening, while Jody and I were fixing something to eat, some Congolese from Yakoma whom Jody knew came rushing up to the house in great excitement.

"The rebels have come to Yakoma!" they shouted.

"What do you mean?"

"Where did they come from?"

Our visitors gathered round. "They came in canoes and scared the soldiers out of the army camp," they said, gesturing with their arms and bodies.

"How many were there?" I asked. We got varying answers: from eight to possibly fifteen. By that time, several more of our Congolese friends had come running up to the house. Each one told us a similar story. Jody and I couldn't make out exactly what had happened, but we became rather frightened, wondering what might have happened to Paul, because he had been due to go into Yakoma that afternoon.

"Have you seen the doctor in town today?" I asked.

"No," they said, shaking their heads.

"Aren't the soldiers chasing the rebels back, if there are so few who crossed the river?"

The Congolese were wild-eyed. "Yes," they said, "the soldiers shoot, but the bullets don't go through! You see, they have *mai na Mulele**—they've put it over their bodies. The bullets don't go in!"

"But this cannot be," we protested. "It is true," our Congolese friends insisted. "We saw it with our own eyes!"

We tried to calm these frightened people despite the mounting fear in our own hearts and despite our anxiety about what really was happening across the river. From our house we could see the Congo side. The trees and the land were clearly visible, but at this juncture of the three rivers—the Uele, the Bili, and the Mbomu where they form the Ubangi—the water is very wide.

By the time we had heard the last of this news, darkness had come and a heaviness had settled on our hearts. We went to bed very disturbed that night, praying that somehow things would work out, that Paul would know the

Mai na Mulele was considered a magic potion. It was water over which a Simba witch doctor had chanted some ritual words. It was reputed to turn bullets to water.

danger that faced him—if there was as much danger as seemed to be lurking all around—and that he might be on his way. Sleep was fitful that night.

Wednesday morning, Paul was on radio as were the other remaining stations. Paul came on with a message, saying:

... There has been a little disturbance here in town. I'm going to check it out before the next call-in time. ... Over.

Jody and I were hearing varying reports from the Congolese who were fleeing across the river. We became greatly alarmed, and wished feverishly that there were some way that we could send a letter across to Paul and tell him that apparently we were getting much more accurate reports from people who were fleeing from Yakoma than he was getting from people around Wasolo station. But there was no way of sending a message. We just had to wait.

The next time we heard Paul, that same afternoon, he was saying:

I must leave this evening. It is time that I leave my station.

We knew that his plans for routes of escape were well formed; at the same time we knew that the most logical of these plans, the easiest of them, would be right down the river through the point from where the trouble came. We now felt, however, that the only time that he could possibly come that way would be in the middle of the night, when nobody would be watching. It could be very dangerous, we knew, no matter what time he came. Another route that he might take would by now be sealed off by rebels if they controlled the road. We had received no satisfactory answers from the fleeing Congolese as to just where the rebels were, just what they were holding, late Wednesday afternoon. We knew that we dared not send a message to Paul. We knew that if anyone was caught with a message his life would be endangered, because we knew the methods that the rebels used, now that we had heard so many reports from their fleeing victims. Furthermore, no one wanted to go back across the river once having fled to the safety of the Central African Republic.

"Now I think I realize how the people in Berlin must feel," I said to Jody, "with the wall separating the parts of the city, with no way of communication across that wall." Our wall was a river. That night we stayed up, waiting and praying, expecting Paul to come at any hour. He did not come that night. Thursday morning he was not on radio, so we felt that he must have left the station. Three stations were still on the air. They did not expect to hear Paul because he had said he was leaving.

Later that morning of Thursday, September 10, we were receiving reports from Congolese coming across the river that the rebels were on their way down to Banzyville. This news gave us great alarm because we thought it might be possible that the rebels had seen Paul and taken him with them. We knew that they would value him as a doctor.

That noon, at regular contact time for our stations, a warning came from official sources of reports from the *gendarmerie* across the river from Banzyville (reports, that is, from the Central African Republic officialdom) that there was trouble in that city, also. This then meant that the Ubangi was in danger throughout its length and breadth. There were still missionaries at Karawa and at Goyongo. Now the message came that all must leave immediately. Those remaining felt they could get their trucks across to Bangui, Central African Republic, so there was an exodus from our field.

Meanwhile, we continued to wait for Paul, to pray for his safety, and to hope that he could somehow get across. Many Congolese by this time had fled across the river, and more were coming every hour. We asked how many rebels there were now, and the answer was, "Many, many." We heard that as many as 2,000 Congolese had fled across the river at Yakoma, but still there was no Paul. We could not imagine what had happened. We did not particularly fear for his life, because the Simbas had not been harming the white people. Yet we did not know where they might have taken him, if they had captured him.

We walked down to the river's edge several times a day, and there we saw the Portuguese *commerçants* from Yakoma, who had fled across the river. One had not even stopped to pick up a change of clothing. In the dash, he had lost his briefcase containing all his valuable papers. These merchants began receiving reports that their stores were being completely dismantled, that the rebels came in and handed over the merchandise for little or nothing, saying, "When we have control, we'll bring you much better merchandise for a much lower price!" They added, "We'll bring lots of new things to the stores!"

The months previously, since independence, had been difficult because there was not a great deal of merchandise in the stores, and what was available was priced high. These rebel promises sounded good to some people. They also promised, "We'll bring you doctors, we'll bring you medicine for your sick," and then they made other great promises. On the other hand, they continued their raiding, their shooting, and their violence. The reports were that they were shooting out every glass window in Yakoma, including the windows in the Catholic church. We stood on shore and peered across. We could see nothing, but we could hear frequent gunshots.

We knew the Portuguese *commerçants* well because during our time at Wasolo we had depended on them for our mail delivery and for bringing produce to us from Bumba, as well as for our purchases in town. Here the men were standing by the river's edge, knowing that all their earthly possessions were being thrown away, that their stores were being ruined in these days when any repair materials were terribly difficult to get. They also knew that their lot in their homeland was not promising. They were a dejected group, and our hearts ached for them. We knew that if the rebels went to our mission station (which seemed at the time unlikely, because the movement was down the road leading to the provincial capital of Gemena, presumably their prime target), we had left some material possessions, yes, and fairly comfortable homes. But we knew that we had loved ones in the States, and many things that we could go home to, if that time came. So material possessions across the river did not count for much to us, as long as Paul came across to us.

One report reached us that a rebel had come to Père Leopold asking him for his motorcycle, and there was nothing to do but give it to the soldier. The rebels were taking all the vehicles in town, anyway. Later on, the story went, the rebel returned to Père Leopold, saying, "Your motorcycle does not run. Will you fix it for me?" As the story goes, after fixing it, Père Leopold said, "Let me try it out before I give it back to you." With that, he took off and made good his escape.

For several hours we hopefully repeated this story among ourselves, but the news changed, and it became clear that Père Leopold was still in Yakoma, although the rebels were not harming the Catholic fathers.

Friday, all Ubangi transmitters were silent. We knew that all of our missionaries had pulled out of the area that was so dear to our hearts. We had tried to prepare our Congolese pastors, leaders, and teachers for such an eventuality, but they did not believe that it could happen. They could not believe that it would happen. How our hearts ached for what might be in store for those we had come to know and love. As Paul had said in his message to our area just a few short weeks before, their faith would have to be strong, their faith in Christ would need to be firm to gird them for their time of trials. We prayed that God would give our Congolese brothers the strength they needed to face their rebel countrymen. Our hearts went out to the wounded, to the mothers unable to give birth without a doctor's assistance, to those who were being left now without medical care, to the boys and girls who should have been starting school that week. Now the missionary teachers had to leave. Congolese teachers fled for their lives because suddenly everyone with an education seemed to be marked for violent death. These youngsters, we knew, would be ready prey for a movement such as the one coming into the Yakoma-Wasolo area. I couldn't help wondering what would happen to the youth in our own country—restless youth without classes, without activities—had they, too, been offered shiny guns and ammunition. This was apparently what was happening just across the river from us.

Shortly before Flossie's wedding, Paul had taped a message to send to our church in the United States. His words came back to me now:

> In days like this we certainly have to leave the future in God's hands. We trust that God will continue to leave an open door. But obviously, whether we will be able to be here, or whether the task will be left to our African Christian brothers, is impossible to say. Continue to uphold us in prayer. Pray that these days of trial may not just be days in which we feel trial, but through the trials we face here we may be an effective witness for Christ. Pray that through the trials being faced by the Congolese Church, we may see growth within the Church, that we may see revival, for we realize that only through revival, a refreshing of the Church, will we receive growth and win Christians who can stand through the problems they are going to have to face in the future. Then pray that we may be able to help them face these problems. It is always

hard to know what to say to them, because they do not realize what has gone on elsewhere in the world. They do not realize that in this century more people have died for their witness for Christ than died in the early centuries, which we think of as the days of martyrs.

We need to prepare them both so they will be willing to suffer if they have to do that to follow Christ, and so that their strength and dependence is truly on him . . . that it might be resting firmly on Christ our Savior so that in times like these they might know that they have a Lord and God who will carry them through.

Thursday . . .

Friday . . .

Saturday morning at five o'clock we heard the cough of gunfire. I had not slept; I bolted upright in bed and called out, "Jody! They've come across the river!" We rushed to the window, but we were assured that the shooting was not on our side of the river, that the vibrations had played a trick and had only sounded as if they were on the shore on our side.

Where was Paul? By the longest route that he had planned, he was long overdue. It was a few minutes after seven o'clock on Saturday morning. I turned on our transistor radio, hoping to get some news over Voice of America. The broadcast was not clear. In turning the dial, I heard a voice. It was a familiar voice. My heart leaped!

"Jody!" I cried. "Come. Help me listen! It's Paul!"

She rushed over and we listened, straining our ears to pick up the words in the confusion of the poor reception. It was the morning hour at which Paul had earlier told us that he would give us personal messages. How we strained our ears to hear! Finally his voice drifted in more clearly:

Lois, Jody, Wayne, and Lyn. I am all right. I am all right. I love you all. Do not stay where you are. Lois, take the children . . . so they may get into school. This may take a long time. I love you.

He sounded so alone. Where was he? We had not heard the call number. Was he possibly at Karawa or Gemena station? Had he been taken captive? And was he able somehow to get on the air while he was captive?

We sat by the radio, listening harder. I prayed out loud: "O Lord, please,

have someone listen in who can respond to him. Please have someone respond!"
Then I heard a transmitter go on. It was another familiar-sounding voice. We
knew all our missionaries were away from their regular stations, yet someone
had heard:

*Dr. Paul, where are you? Everyone is gone. You are the only one remaining.
Where are you?*

The answer came: *Nine-Q-Three-Nine. Three-Nine is here.*

With that, we knew he was calling from our own station, from Wasolo. He
continued:

*I'm sorry I've misjudged the situation. I'm here. Please get plane reservations
for the family and Jody so they may leave the area that they are in.*

And what about you? Can we send in a plane or a copter?

Paul responded slowly: *No, please don't. If I leave in such a way, they may
harm others. Please don't. I'm all right now. I'm sure things will work out. Do
not expect me to respond again today. I am all right. The Lord is very near.*

With that the transmitter clicked off. Our prayer that we would know where
he was had been answered. We did not want to leave the area where we were
so close to him, and yet we knew that we must. We knew that the children
must get to school—wherever it might be for the remaining missionary children. We could not find out then because we had no means to send a message.
We had tried the afternoon before sending a telegram to Bangui to our missionaries there, but we found that the telegraph office was closed and would
remain closed for the weekend. We knew we had to get to the town of Bangassou
in order to get a plane to Bangui.

Jody sent a message by runner to a coffee plantation owner nearby whom
we knew, a Frenchman, asking if he by chance had an errand in Bangassou on
Monday. The reply came back, "Yes, I have. I'll be glad to take you there."

Our hearts were heavy. We kept praying that somehow Paul would find a
way to come across and we wouldn't have to leave the area without him. On
Sunday refugees from Yakoma still streamed across, and we had news from
them that they had seen the doctor in Yakoma on Saturday afternoon treating
the wounded. They said that apparently he had been asked to come, that he
was well, but that they had not been able to get near enough to him to obtain

any message. They had just seen him as they were fleeing. We did not understand what was going on, but at least we had word that he had been seen, and that his truck had returned to the Wasolo station.

Monday came. We had made arrangements to leave Kemba. Paul had come on radio at regular contact time with a message saying that he was well and that he felt things would quiet down so that he would be able to come, but did not feel that the time had yet come that he could leave in such a way. It was with heavy hearts that we packed our things into the plantation owner's jeep, climbed in, and left. In Kemba we left a camp cot and a trunk with food and some changes of clothing, so that Paul, in the event he got across, would have some supplies.

About halfway to Bangassou we asked the French planter what his errand was in town that day. "To take you folks there," he said.

We were his reason for going to town! During our days at Kemba he had sent messengers frequently to ask if there was anything we needed. And when we arrived at Bangassou he would take no pay for the difficult three-hour drive. Here was a fresh example of the eagerness of people to help us in our hour of need.

The Baptist Mid-Mission in Bangassou had received a telegram from a missionary saying we were on our way and so they expected us and gave us a warm welcome. In fact, they were on the point of setting out to look for us when we arrived. We were to take a plane from there to Bangui the next morning, but delays arose and we spent two nights and a day at Bangassou. The mission is situated close to the river. We were told not to be alarmed if we heard jeeps driving through the mission during the night. They were keeping up a patrol because of the nearness of the Congo rebel forces. We were in the Central African Republic, but with just a river between, it would not have been too difficult for a few rebels to cross should they decide to be brave. Threats they were shouting could be heard on our side of the river, so at that point the Simbas seemed too close for comfort. These shouts put great fear in the hearts of the Africans on our side. At a nearby village, the inhabitants became very scared, saying, "The rebels are coming in the morning, and we are afraid."

"There are soldiers to stop the Simbas," the Baptist missionaries reassured them.

"But soldiers cannot stop them. Bullets cannot go through them!"

The missionaries explained that this was witchcraft and that of course the bullets could go through, and that the soldiers could guard the border; but the Africans did not seem convinced.

Wednesday morning the plane arrived, and Jody, the children, and I got aboard for Bangui. We were reluctant to go, and I had difficulty in controlling the tears, but I told myself that it was particularly for the children's sake that we went. I could not put the date out of mind: September 16. It was our fourteenth wedding anniversary, and I was going farther away from Paul.

After a two-hour flight over the dense jungle and over part of the Ubangi area, we arrived in Bangui to be greeted there by our missionaries. We were welcomed into the "refugee camp," as it was called, at the Brethren Mission. There were twenty-six "refugee" missionaries there. We were later assigned to a house that was rented by our mission and we brought the refugee number in that house to fourteen. Among them were the Monsons and the Lindquists. It was good in many ways to be together, because we had found that there is a strong bond among missionaries—a bond that to us sometimes seems stronger than family bonds. Often to outsiders the bond is hard to understand, yet at a time like this there had to be no prodding, no questions asked, just the comfort of being together and praying together as a group. Wayne and Lyn were very happy to be reunited with the children they knew and had been going to school with, so this bond was not limited to grownups alone. It was possible to notify Paul of our safe arrival in Bangui.

In Bangassou I had met a Norwegian doctor who had been captured in Stanleyville and then released. He felt that no harm would be done to Paul; that the rebels would realize his value and worth. Someone suggested sending a helicopter in, but on second thought it was realized that the distance was too great without a refueling station. Also, a small airplane had no place to land at Wasolo. The river seemed so near, all the time; it still seemed to be the perfect escape route.

We knew there could be danger in any type of rescue for Paul. We realized that in times like those, one could never be sure who might be around when, or who might be the enemy. We knew that farther inland in Congo at an earlier date, a pilot had been killed in trying to make a rescue with a small plane. We knew the terrain of Wasolo. The most sensible thing seemed to be for Paul to get out by the water route at the time he felt to be best. We knew it might also be dangerous to insist on radio communication with him, because the diesel motor had to be turned on. The motor house, sitting on top of the hill, could be heard for a great distance. We knew that the rebels were suspicious of any type of radio equipment, binoculars, hearing aids—just about anything of that sort they regarded as a "phonee," or short-wave radio. There could not be anything secret about the Wasolo motor being on—whether it was for electricity for things around the house or for power for transmitting purposes.

Friday morning, September 18, Paul came on the air briefly to tell us that he was all right. He knew of course that we were terribly concerned for him, and if we did not hear from him we would be very worried. But he said he felt that he could not come on the air at times that we might expect, and for us not to be unduly concerned if he didn't come on. Also, he might very possibly be operating at the hospital, and for that reason could not come on the air.

We kept listening at every contact hour that had been appointed. Paul never came on again.

After a few days, a report from the Kemba area said that the rebels had gone to Wasolo; that they had taken the doctor and some priests from Yakoma across the two rivers—the Uele and the Bili; that they had built barges of some sort in order to take vehicles across. This indeed was dreadful news, for we did not know where Paul might be taken or what manner of treatment they would show him and those who were with him. There was absolutely no means of contact from the area they were reportedly going into.

We prayed that God would protect Paul; that the necessary things for life would somehow be given to him; and that his own faith and strength would hold up during these trials that he was going through.

After hearing this report of Paul's capture, one of the American embassy officials took the long route up to the Kemba area on the Central African

Republic side of the Ubangi River to check out the reports and to see if anything could be done to rescue Paul. Along the way the official's vehicle overturned, but fortunately, there was no injury to him or to his chauffeur. Somehow they righted the car, and drove on. They questioned the Congolese who had fled across from Yakoma. It was learned then that on September 23, Paul and three priests had been taken across the Uele and Bili rivers by truck on hastily built barges into the Monga area. It was reported that they were taking them to Stanleyville. There was some report of a trial, also, at this time. These threats, we were told, were not unusual, but naturally they caused us a great deal of concern.

We heard then that the people of our area screamed in protest as they took their doctor, Monganga Paul, away. They loved him. They needed him. They did not want any harm to come to him.

From Kemba offers of ransom for the doctor's safe return were reportedly rejected. There seemed to be nothing at this time that could be done. There were also reports that two had been killed at the hospital, and soon we heard that one of our Congolese nurses and one of the station workers had been killed. We wondered especially about the fate of Vuku, Gebanga Joseph, and Wanzi, our trusted friends. Several days later, we heard that they had escaped, but with some minor injuries, and we were thankful that they had been spared, as they provided a true backbone for the work of the mission at Wasolo.

In a letter home at this time, I wrote: "These are difficult days for our family. We are finding the Lord's strength sufficient for each day, and only are able to take a day at a time. Who could ever dream of being in such a situation?"

I refused to go back to the United States, feeling that being in Bangui, near to the American embassy, would provide me as quickly as possible with any news that might leak out. Also, in this city I was as near as I could possibly be to where Paul was.

It came time, then, for the children to start school. There were ten missionary children remaining and room was found for them in a classroom, with dormitory space, at the Brethren Mission about 200 miles north of Bangui. Wayne was well accustomed to dormitory life by this time and agreed to go with the children to school. It would have been the first time for Lyn, and she did not want to go.

"Mommy, I feel just like a little kitten that is being taken away from its mommy too soon," she said to me. With these words I did not have the heart to send her away to school. Permission was given by her teacher for the books to be loaned to me, and I continued teaching her, this time second-grade subjects.

It was a great comfort to have at least one of our children with me, even though I felt that I wasn't being a very conscientious teacher during those days; but Lyn was an eager and able student, which probably made up for my inadequacy. Our refugee camp was thinning out with each passing day, and many of the missionaries were being assigned with either the Baptist or Brethren stations. Others, including Jody, who were due furlough time, went on home to the States.

Lynette and I continued living in the house with Jim and Polly Monson and their two little ones. The four Lindquist children had joined the others in school, and Frank and Margaret spent a few days at another station before returning to live in the house next door to the one I was living in, in Bangui. It was a great comfort to have them so near.

At the very end of September a notice came from the State Department saying that Paul was in Stanleyville at work in a hospital there. This did not jibe with the length of time I knew it took to get from our area to Stanleyville. I began receiving letters from people in the States saying that they were glad their prayers had been answered for Paul because he was safe and working in Stanleyville. These letters upset me because I felt that the reports had not been true, and I wrote home asking the people to pray for Paul because we did not know at all where he was, despite these reports.

The days passed slowly. October came and began to slip by until, in late October, in a letter home I wrote of a report that we had received from the American embassy—a report that had come in a roundabout way, but as all sources had been listed, we tended to credit it. The report said that Paul and the three priests had been released at Buta. "I don't want to get my hopes up too high," I wrote to the family, "but just pray that this is a true report. If you only knew the lack of communication systems out here, you would realize why it is so hard to find out anything. I don't think people in the States can have any idea. This report was heard over the Brussels radio by some of our Congolese friends in Gemena, also. It came out of Congo by a Congolese priest and then was relayed to Antwerp. This report does sound logical ... [in contrast to some of the discrepancies in the report from Stanleyville]."

I also became fearful of things that were being printed in the papers back home. I became fearful of my own mail being opened. I stopped putting my name on letters. I used only my box number. It wasn't a very comfortable feeling. About this time, the third week in October, several of our men missionaries had received permission to go back into the Ubangi for a few days. Working on the assumption that Paul was released at Buta, two of the men, Frank Lindquist and Bob Thornbloom, decided they would very cautiously make the trip to Wasolo to see if they could gather more information as to what had happened, what might be happening, and to find out if they could possibly get into the area where Paul was reportedly released.

They didn't tell us women of their intentions, and only on their return did they tell me that they had spent my birthday—October 27—at Wasolo. Frank told about the trip to Wasolo as they crept along the road gauging the safety of proceeding further every few miles. They were told to put a white cloth around the truck so that on sight the villagers would know they were on a friendly mission. The villagers were on guard and cautious. Any truck approaching the area was a natural cause of suspicion among the Congolese. After all they had been through, one could hardly blame them.

As the men got to Wasolo, people came running out excitedly, for the truck they were in was almost identical to the one we had had at Wasolo. Before even looking to see who was in the truck, they threw their arms about Bob, crying, "Monganga Paul has come back!" Then they realized that it was not Paul, but Frank and Bob, who were looking for him, seeking information as to his whereabouts.

Another village near to Wasolo had been completely destroyed, they learned. They were shown a grave where thirty had been buried. Fear and sadness were written in the faces and in the eyes of the people; they had been through so much. On arrival at Wasolo hospital itself, Frank and Bob looked around and found that doors and windows had been broken. They saw the place where one of our nurses, Bomba Boniface, and a hospital worker, Constant Kokembe, had been killed. There were bullet holes in the walls.

They went up the hill to our house. The house was standing, but on the inside it was in shambles. Papers from the filing cabinets, and feathers from the pillows were strewn all over the floor. Beds, furniture, dishes, food, everything had been taken. All locked doors had been broken. In talking to the people Frank and Bob learned some of what had happened, but accurate dates and events are hard to piece together, and much of what came out from their trip probably cannot be precisely verified. But it was learned that things had remained quiet at Wasolo for several days, without actual intrusion by the rebels. Then, apparently, a Congolese nurse (who had not been trained in mission hospitals) who had once worked at the Wasolo hospital, and had been discharged from his duties before we were ever there, had gone to the local rebel command and told them that the doctor had a "phonee." The rebels did come then, demanding to know where the "phonee" was. A report was that this former nurse slapped Paul across the face with a hard blow. Our yard worker, Kanga Joseph, who had been a faithful helper but was of a very simple nature, when threatened with his life, said, "I'll tell you where the doctor's transmitter and radio are, if you'll let me loose." When I reflect on his answer I wonder what some of us might say if we had a gun poking us in the back, and our life or death depended on our words.

Paul then was taken away from Wasolo in our own mission truck. Frank and Bob found that there was no way they could safely go over to the area where Paul had been reportedly taken. So, after collecting what information they could, and taking a few papers they had found on the floor that they thought I might value, they returned.

There was fighting just sixty kilometers away, at Wapinda, at the time they made this visit, so they did not dare stay very long—only over one night.

Now, in the months since these events, I have received letters from several Catholic priests and several of our dear Congolese friends, and have been able to piece together some of the things that went on during those days that we were in the dark. A letter from Gebanga Joseph gives what I am sure is an accurate picture of events. His letter says:

> On the eighth of September at 2 p.m., the doctor, Wanzi, and others went to see you again, but on the way they heard gun-firing in the camp of the soldiers, so they stopped to ask about it. They were told that the rebels were fighting the soldiers of the Congolese National Army, so they came back to the mission, saying it was not wise to go to Kemba as if they were fleeing. . . .
>
> I told them I would go into Yakoma to see with my own eyes what was happening. So in the morning I and one of the nurses went as far as the Catholic mission. There we saw the rebels come and take the truck belonging to Père Leopold, to take more rebels to the crossroad at Ngunde to overtake the soldiers there.
>
> We returned at eleven in the morning and told the doctor to pack his things and tell the other missionaries that he was going to be leaving. He agreed and we told Vuku to come in the boat so we could go by water. It was about 9 p.m. and we were leaving and someone came with a letter from Père Leopold saying that the rebels asked for the doctor to come and help the wounded from the battle.
>
> Dr. Paul said, "All right. I will not leave." He told us that no one had done him any wrong. He knew that we wanted to save him, but it was not God's will that he go. So I told him that I knew he wanted to stay with us, but it would be well for him to go. If he did not want to go to Kemba, he could go with me into the forest. We could take food and make a grass house there. He refused this, saying it would not be bad for him to go, but if he went, the people he had operated on would die, and if the rebels heard that he had left, they would kill all of us.
>
> On Friday, September 11, we received a letter from the chief of the rebels saying that they wanted to see the doctor the next day. They wanted him to come with medicine and the mission people to come with food. That night I again told the doctor that we should go to Kemba, but he did not want to go.
>
> On September 12, Saturday, we all went in with chickens and peanuts

and plantains, and Wanzi took a goat. The teachers and nurses and some of the lepers and many people from the mission went with us. Dr. Paul told me to get off the truck and stay to watch the mission. He chose Vuku to stay with me.

I began to cry. He said that if I cried he would not go, and if he did not go, the rebels would come and kill everyone. He put his arms around me, and prayed and went. They left at 8 a.m. and did not return until 5:30 p.m. The rebels said they could do no harm to Dr. Paul because he was a doctor and was healing people, but that night when we were eating—just the two of us in his house—he said to me that his heart was heavy, and that it would be well if we prayed a little. He read Matthew 26:42: "He went away a second time, and prayed: 'My Father, if it is not possible for this cup to pass me by without my drinking it, thy will be done.'" Then, I had no more words to convince him. He told me he was going to contact Lois and tell her to go to Bangui with the children so they could go to school.

On September 15 the rebels sent a letter asking him for medicine. On September 18 the rebels came to Wasolo. They went into the hospital and they began to shoot. They asked for no one. When they shot, Bomba fell down and Kokembe also, and everyone began to run behind the building.

We began to run, too. At that time, Paul heard the shooting, and came out of the medical-surgical room where he had been visiting his patients who had just gone through surgery. The rebels captured him along with Père Leopold, Père Monulphe, and another *père*, who had come from Molegbe to visit them. They were all in the truck. The rebels had taken them from Yakoma. They went on up the hill and began to break windows and doors and to destroy things in your house. They burned some and began to put things in their truck.

When they had destroyed everything on the hill, in the school, and in the hospital, they took the doctor and the priests to Wapinda. There they destroyed the hospital and the houses belonging to the priests.

I have received letters from two of the priests who had been injured at Wapinda. They had been beaten severely; one was very seriously injured. Paul persuaded the Simbas that these injured priests, especially the one, could not be taken away because they could not stand the trip, and would certainly die. Paul said, "You cannot leave two injured priests alone, but you must leave one to care for them."

These priests have written grateful letters, which I treasure, and one such letter, from Père Prosper tells of these events:

"Having been mistreated myself at Wapinda on the 16th of September, it was the doctor himself, with his truck, who was forced, on the 18th of September, under the surveillance of the [rebel] army, to take us to Yakoma from Wapinda. During three days we were prisoners together, the doctor and six priests. The doctor himself was able to obtain from the rebel chiefs the permission to care for Father Gideon and me, having received fractures and wounds caused by mistreatment. They were sent to Bondo the 21st of September. Thanks to the doctor, we were able to remain at Yakoma, and thus were liberated by the National Congolese Army the 22nd of September."

Gebanga Joseph says that Paul remained a prisoner at Yakoma for five days. Joseph and Wanzi and some of their friends stayed in the forests nearby waiting to see if Paul would be set free. When the rebels took him away across the Uele and Bili rivers, they did not stay in the forests any longer, but crossed the Ubangi River to Kemba.

In a letter to me, Matthieu Bangi, the pastor at Wasolo, tells of how he fled into the jungle along with several children, some other men and women, and made a small place for themselves to hide, like hunted animals:

"Truly the Yakoma people received much difficulty from the rebels. However, because God is a God of wisdom and strength he sent them soldiers of the Congolese National Army. Had these soldiers not come, the entire population would have been wiped out."

On the 23rd, Pastor Bangi came out of hiding to find what news there was. He heard of the killings and the violence, and he saw much of the killing by the townspeople of Yakoma of the rebels before the Nationalist soldiers came to take up that task themselves. He tells how the people of the neighboring village of Targini came and asked if Bangi would come and stay with them.

Paul by the 23rd had been taken to Bondo along with Père Leopold, Père Monulphe, and Père Adrian. Between there and Buta they were badly mistreated, beaten, driven, ridiculed, made to cut grass with long blades without protective handles, so their hands became very sore. In a brief diary of Paul's that was returned to me, he has a notation for that day that reads simply, "Saved by God."

They were in Buta for a time and it seems that the reports were true that for about four weeks they enjoyed relative freedom. There Paul stayed at the Catholic mission. I have received three letters written by Paul at this time and left with the fathers who, he felt, might be released before he was. These letters have come to me by roundabout ways. The last two arrived as long afterward as July 1965. There are no descriptions of the events taking place, but he mentions how good the fathers of the mission were being to him, and what wonderful fellowship he was having with them, especially with Père Leopold.

In a letter dated September 24 he wrote:

Forgive me for the worry I have caused. I was wrong to try to stay, but I feel I put it all into God's hands and must leave it there. I have learned with the Apostle Paul "For me to live is Christ and die is gain" at times. We thought that time had come several times during the last week since we were taken. We have seen beatings and other things, but God is always gracious. I am in good health without injury of consequence. Pray not for deliverance but for my testimony. That's why I am here. I'm learning to wait on the Lord, but I have much to learn. For me to live and die is gain—this becomes more real each day. I've had beatings and known what it means not to know the future for tomorrow. Where I go to from here I know not, only that it will be with Him. If by God's grace I live, which I doubt, it will be to His glory. But remember, things like this indicate the power of the adversary and mean we should all work harder for Christ. So few of us learn the road to follow Him. I'm learning as I go but there are valleys. Yes, this sort of thing indicates failure on the part of us Christians in spreading the Gospel, also. But remember the church never grows in plenty but in time of martyrdom.

I trust for revival in Ubangi. I pray for such. God guide each and pray with me that each day we live for Him we might be a witness.

So many times during those days of waiting in Bangui I wondered if perchance Paul had his New English Version New Testament with him, which he liked to read. He would always read a portion before breakfast, then leave the Testament on the coffee table. He never took it with him to the hospital. It was in English and would serve no purpose in reading to the patients or anyone else. It was merely for his own reading. So he had no reason to have it with him, but still I wondered.

By some miracle he did have it with him, I later learned, and this small volume provided countless hours of comfort to him. During this time in his reading of it, he underlined and made notations in the margins, a habit of his when reading anyway. A letter from Father Slegers, of the Catholic mission at Buta, says, "Dr. Carlson remained a whole month at our mission at Buta. We accepted him as one of our own in Christ. We admired his courage, his kindness, his simplicity, and his faith. He occupied the room next to mine. Often I found him meditating on the New Testament which he always had with him. When he left, as we embraced, he said to me, 'Let us pray much.'"

For approximately four weeks things were calm at Buta, permitting some rest for the weary prisoners. At one time Paul apparently thought he could go back to Yakoma, but was kept from doing so. About this time most of the vehicles in the area had been run down or confiscated, and that meant none of them was reliable on the bumpy roads. The danger was ever present along the roads, as the rebel forces controlled them. Paul was not known by the villagers in that area either. The three priests from the Yakoma mission, Pères Leopold, Adrian, and Monulphe, were taken from Buta back to, it was thought, the Bondo area. Paul was left at Buta.

There was not much for him to do while he was at this mission. There were no medicines for him to treat anyone with. Paul loved to read, but there is no way of telling how much he got out of the French-language books that were around that area.

The National Congolese Army, along with the mercenaries, had come as far as Bumba and had liberated that town. Our hopes increased as we heard this news in Bangui, and I kept praying that if Paul was at Buta, he would be next to be released. His hopes were along this line also. At Buta they knew that Bumba had been liberated. They felt that they were in line next.

They waited.

We waited.

To Buta came a visitor, the self-appointed president of the rebels, Christophe Gbenye. Somehow Paul's presence was brought to his attention. They were looking for mercenaries; they were seeking to capture a mercenary. Did it matter if this were a missionary? The words in French for the two do not differ much—*mercenaire* and *missionnaire*. Not too great a difference in sound. Perhaps the person did not matter too much either. Paul was unknown in this area. So, on October 21, Paul was taken to Stanleyville. Before leaving, he scribbled a brief will and a letter, which he left with a priest there. This letter found its way to me at the end of December. It read in part:

Once again, I had hopes that it would be soon over, and now I have to go to Stan. It is difficult to understand all the reasons, but I have a good escort and that means a lot. Also the fact that I'm a doctor seems to be a help. It's a big disappointment, but I can only do what I have done all along—put my trust in God. We realize our little faith at a time like this, but it is good for us to have to put all our trust in Him and not rely on ourselves. God has given me many blessings, and I am holding Him to such promises as are found in 2 Timothy 4:17, 18: "I was rescued out of the lion's jaws, and the Lord will rescue me from every attempt to do me harm." And from Acts 27:24, "Do not be afraid, Paul . . . keep up your courage." Yet I wouldn't be human if there weren't fear. I know I'm ready to meet my Lord but my thoughts for you make all this more difficult. I trust that I might be a witness for Christ. I know that you are praying that I might be that. I can only realize when I see such difficulties as we have seen that we need to work all the harder for our Lord. I'm praying that through this we might see revival in our churches in the Ubangi, in the hearts of all of us, and our Congolese brothers, too. For each of those at Yakoma I am continually in prayer that God will protect them in these difficult days and strengthen them in faith.

A brief message was included in the letters for each member of the family. To his mother and dad Paul wrote, "You gave me to God—leave me there and find your peace in Him. I am confident of His direction."

Paul's Testament continued to be a source of strength. He was making a notation in it one day when his rebel guard took the Testament, pulled out the page, and then unaccountably returned the Testament to Paul. The road to Stanleyville was to be dangerous, painful, cruel, and long.

X

November

The days in Bangui seemed endless. How could this go on and on and on, I asked myself. Waking during the night, I would pray for God to watch over Paul. He alone knew where Paul was. During this time we received a copy of the *Baltimore Sunday Sun*, with the article about Phil Littleford, and with references throughout to Paul and the work at Wasolo.

We had wondered when it would be published, and strangely enough, the date turned out to be Sunday, September 6. It was the day—the last day—we had seen Paul.

This story was picked up by the Los Angeles papers, with the focus on Paul's work at the mission hospital. Scarcely two weeks later, reports of Paul's capture appeared in these same papers. "Local Medic Capured" the headlines said. Many of these articles disturbed me because they seemed to have a wrong slant on what was truly our story. I became more and more concerned as to their possible effect on Paul if these reports were circulated.

By early November, I had become the missionary who received the largest stack of mail on mail day. The letters comforted me with their words of encouragement, with their messages of assurance that many people were praying for us. Letters came from persons of all faiths, telling us of their prayers for Paul. How I wished that Paul could have seen some of these letters, to bolster his own morale. Yet I knew somehow that he would feel all these prayers for him.

Still the time dragged by. *Where was Paul?* That question kept tormenting me, and we were hearing nothing. One night, over Voice of America, we heard the news of American missionary William Scholten's death. Our hearts were saddened, and we also knew that the place of his death was very near the area to which Paul had been taken.

Of course, our daily life continued. We were still living with our friends in Bangui. I was teaching Lynette her second-grade classes. It was difficult to write, as I did every few days, to Wayne at school, to say that there was still no news of Daddy. The needs of our own bodies had to be met, and it was particularly difficult to think of preparing food. I couldn't look at food without wondering whether Paul had anything to eat. I prayed: "O Lord, provide food for him. Keep him well, and strengthen his faith."

One day I received a letter from Wanzi, who had fled across the river to Kemba: "We are praying God that He will take care of Dr. Paul in the hands of evil men. We are sitting in sorrow and we are very lonely. Do not forget God."

And from Wanzi's brother Gebanga Joseph: "I want to say to you, Mrs. Carlson, that you should not be overcome with sorrow, for even though it is truly a heartache, we are all children of the Lord God who knows all things, whether sorrow or joy, whether happiness or grief. Just pray together with us that God will be with Dr. Paul, and that we will all see him again."

It was a great comfort to have these letters, and it was also good to hear that many of our people who had fled across the river were such faithful Christians. As one of the missionaries near Kemba said, they were truly "shining lights." We also sorrowed with these people, knowing that they were hungry, that they had left their gardens and what little clothing they had, and fled. They, too, were in a foreign country. It was hard for them without money or means of livelihood.

On October 26, Radio Stanleyville announced that a Major Carlson, a mercenary, had been brought to Stanleyville and would stand trial as a spy. I discussed this with the American embassy staff in Bangui. This was not a new accusation against Americans, I was told, and the feeling was that if Paul was in Stanleyville, he would at least be with other Americans. We knew that five American consulate men were being held, along with many American missionaries. I knew that Paul would be very glad to be with others who spoke his language and that possibly food would be a little easier to obtain in that city.

On the Voice of America broadcast of October 28, the announcement that Radio Stanleyville had made was repeated. I shuddered to think that now our name was in the world news. It was a ridiculous accusation. Paul had spent twenty-two months in the Navy when he was a boy of eighteen. Since that time he had had no connection whatever with the military. Why would they label him "Major"? He was a doctor and a missionary, nothing else. Couldn't his captors understand that? Why were they using Paul Carlson's name and not one of the other hostages?

Then again there was a period of virtual silence. For three weeks we wondered what the result of the so-called trial of "Major Carlson" was. There was no news, and again the tormenting questions assailed me. Was Paul actually in Stanleyville? Was he alive? Radio Stanleyville announced only what they wanted to announce and at times that suited them. About this time the accusations against Americans and Belgians in general were stepped up.

Reports that Americans and Belgians, including missionaries, were being killed, began to come through. Supposedly, according to reports, an order had been issued saying that any mercenaries found be brought to the rebel leaders, but that the order had been misunderstood and all *missionaries* had been brought to Simba headquarters. No one knew, however, and no one could confirm any of the reports that were being broadcast. No one knew what was going on.

Slowly the days edged on. I tried as best I could to keep on a regular schedule, to keep Lyn involved in her lessons, and to preserve the most normal conditions that could be maintained under the circumstances.

Monday, November 16, brought the startling news that "Major Carlson" had been tried and was facing execution. When the news came to me, I cried aloud, "What can we do? What can we do? Can't somebody do something?" At the moment, our band of missionaries and I knew that we were absolutely powerless, in ourselves, to do anything. Frank said, "We can pray." As we bowed our heads in prayer, we felt the nearness of God, in a way that I had never experienced before.

Wayne had come home for a weekend visit, and it was decided that he would stay with us. He joined us at prayer time, and said, "I want you to read the 27th Psalm. We've been studying it, and learning it at school. The verse that really strikes me is the last verse." We read it: "Wait on the LORD: be of good courage, and he shall strengthen thine heart: wait, I say, on the LORD."

Late that night, after hours of anguished prayer, I felt very tired, and yet I did not want to go to bed. Then the thought came to me clearly: "Get some rest. You will need your strength. The people back home are awake and praying." I tumbled, exhausted, into bed. The hours were now endless. On the wall of my room was a poem by Annie Johnson Flint, sent to me by one of our missionaries:

> One day at a time, but the day is so long,
> And the heart is not brave, and the soul is not strong;
> O thou pitiful Christ, be Thou near all the way,
> Give courage and patience and strength for the day.
> Swift cometh His answer, clear and so sweet,
> "Yea, I will be with thee, thy trouble to meet;
> I will not forget thee nor fail thee nor grieve,
> I will not forsake thee, I never will leave."

Our missionary circle continued with the necessary daily tasks: shopping for food, mending, washing, cleaning. No one said much because no one had to. Each of us knew the others were in almost continual silent prayer. I received a telegram from the Covenant Department of World Missions in Chicago saying that they were holding special prayer sessions for Paul. The executive secretary of world missions, Dr. Arden Almquist, gave a message for Voice of America, and the next evening, in the heart of Africa, we heard Paul's brother,

Dwight. How close was our bond though we were thousands of miles apart! It was a comfort to us all.

The members of the American embassy staff were like part of our family. Our sorrows, our fears became their sorrows and fears. I wrote home saying that I knew I was in the best place possible for me because of the warmth in the missionary circle, and because of the interest of the embassy staff. Their advice was that I should stop listening to the radio so much. I tried to follow that advice. The constant repetition of the same news was terribly wearing to one's emotions. I also found that I was being protected from the press. I had no idea what our families at home were going through, especially Paul's family. I only prayed that the Lord would give them strength, that Mom Carlson, with a known heart condition, would be able to withstand the pressures of these days, for I knew that Paul would feel very bad if something were to happen to her because of what was happening to him.

It wasn't until the weekend of November 21 that the *Time-Life* reporters were allowed to come to our house for an interview along with a member of the French press. No one else was allowed. Of course, having outsiders around the house at a time like this was most difficult. We were told to go about our tasks as normally as possible. Wayne and Lynette grew weary of pictures being snapped, but were cooperative. I just didn't care what was going on. My thoughts were elsewhere.

There were reports in the news about negotiations that were to take place at Nairobi, Kenya; that the rebels were sending a representative, Kanza, to Nairobi. Dr. Carlson was being used as a tool in these negotiations. If the rebel leaders did not get their wishes they threatened to take his life. The United States and Belgium had paratroopers ready to drop on Stanleyville to protect the hostages if negotiations weren't successful. Then came the report that Kanza didn't arrive. "How can anyone negotiate with a group that doesn't even have a representative show up?" I thought. It was heartrending, when we knew so many lives were hanging in the balance, that our loved one's name was being used as a tool.

I was asked to tape a message to be given over the radio station at Bangui. I stated that Paul was a doctor and a missionary and nothing else; that he had no connection at all with anything military or political; that he had come to help the Congolese; and, I asked, would they now release him to those who needed him and loved him?

Monday afternoon the American ambassador himself brought me the encouraging news that Radio Stanleyville had said that Paul Carlson was alive and well, as were the other hostages. Our spirits rose. Yet with the news of the paratroopers in readiness for the Stanleyville drop to rescue the hostages and with negotiations proceeding very slowly, the cloud of uncertainty hung heavy upon us. Again, the missionaries in our small community prayed far into the night. We had the assurance that the Lord was watching over Paul.

Early Tuesday morning, November 24, we had our radios on. News came that at that moment paratroopers were dropping from planes onto Stanleyville. I ran next door, where Frank and Margaret were staying, and said, "Today is the day. I hope they know what they're doing and who is there!"

The road to Stanleyville was rough for Paul, as I later learned. And he thought that his end had come. In a letter from Mary Rutt, a missionary who worked with LECO, a Christian bookstore and publisher in Stanleyville, she tells of how the five missionaries living in the LECO apartments heard of Paul at the prison from a small piece of paper with his name printed on it, asking them to send food for him.

They didn't know who he was, and then later in the day, October 23, Mel Loewen, of the Protestant University, stopped in and told them more about Paul. How sorry they were to hear that another missionary was a prisoner. Before that an Africa Inland Mission couple, Chuck and Muriel Davis, and their two children had spent some time with the LECO personnel. Mary Rutt tells how they had suffered at the hands of the rebels, how they had been separated for several weeks, and how Muriel Davis and the children stayed at the LECO apartment. Meantime, on such people as these the prisoners depended for food.

Relatives and friends were permitted to bring food in, and the missionaries at LECO had been assigned to bring food for the white prisoners at the time. The day after Paul's arrival in Stanleyville, he was transferred to the Palace Hotel, which was a rather nice place. The LECO people had not been told of this, so his food went to the prison. Later in the afternoon, Paul was feeling hungry, so he talked his guard into permitting him to go to the LECO apartment to get something to eat. His guard was a nice fellow who was a Simba by constraint, and was hoping to get out of it himself, sometime.

Paul arrived about three o'clock on Saturday afternoon and introduced himself. As Mary writes, "We were happy to see him, and be able to help him, but he arrived in the midst of a flood." She had turned on the water in the bathroom and had forgotten it. It had flooded into the living room, so Paul found them in the midst of mopping up.

He stayed at the apartment for supper. For the next four days he was permitted to come to them at mealtimes. He was enjoying his room at the hotel as much as possible, under the circumstances. Of course his guard was always with him. Paul told them at LECO how much he enjoyed being with them, and how much the fellowship meant to him. He was beginning to relax and to get back his appetite; he had lost a lot of weight.

During this comparative freedom, he met a number of the Unevangelized Fields Missions missionaries, and also the British vice-consul, who was going to work for his release. The Sunday Paul was in the LECO apartment, the British vice-consul came to see him. He had injured his knee. Paul examined it and gave him orders to try to stay off it. The guard who had come with Paul watched very closely. Mary Rutt writes, "I wondered what he thought. It certainly was proof to him that he really was a doctor."

Mary tells a little of the nature of some conversations and that they preferred not to discuss the troubles around them. Paul did say that he wanted to get back to his hospital, back to his own people! He had been forced to witness some of the executions, had seen his own helpers killed and that was hard on him.

"He was thinking of you on your birthday, he mentioned it often and said how much he wished he could be with you. He mentioned the children, too, and told us their ages. I am sure he was living for the day when he would see you all again," Mary writes. "We all expected he would be released when it became known that he was a missionary."

There was one heartening incident while he was a prisoner at the hotel. A

Simba from the region of Wasolo heard that he was in Stanleyville and went to see him. The soldier was glad to see Paul, because, as he told his companions, Dr. Carlson had saved the life of a member of his family. The Simba said he would speak to the colonel and assure him that Dr. Carlson was a missionary. This gave Paul some encouragement.

After a few days, Paul's guard told the LECO people that Paul had been put back in prison, and his food was again sent to him there. That day was the first of the mass arrests of Americans and Belgians—men, women, and children. Chuck Davis was taken prisoner for a second time.

Mary goes on to say, "From this time on until evacuation, we did all we could for them: washed and ironed their clothes, sent them blankets, and bug bombs, and so forth. We were permitted to do this although we were not allowed to communicate with them. Paul was with the American consul and his four aides, two Pax Boys,* the Belgian consul and his aide, the Italian consul, and the director of the Railroad between Stanleyville and Ponthierville. These prisoners were our special charges. Other 'free' white people sent food to the other prisoners."

Mary continues, "Had it not been for him and all the propaganda about him, I do not think people would have realized our situation in Stanleyville. How hopeless it seemed at times, though we knew the Lord was with us, and in His time He would work it all out—according to His will. Paul took care of the medical needs of the other prisoners. He wrote on a piece of paper drugs he needed, and sent it to us. We would phone the pharmacy and they would send the medicine. The director of the Railroad had been under treatment for a stomach ulcer before he was arrested, and I'm afraid his environment did not contribute anything to his well-being. They needed a doctor in their midst."

Paul was calm and helped to ease the fears of the prisoners. He taught some of them how to play games to pass the time and became good friends with the Italian consul. He and two Mennonite prisoners (the Pax Boys), Gene Bergman and Jon Snyder, read their Bibles, studied, and had prayer together. Several of

*Pax Boys was the name given to Gene Bergman and Jon Snyder, Mennonite conscientious objectors who were also being held prisoner.

the other prisoners became interested in the Bible studies and prayer. They were impressed with Paul's faith. Though Paul never forced his beliefs on anyone, he was always ready with an answer to questions. Gene Bergman later said, "Many were touched by his radiant testimony and all were amazed at his calm during all that was going on. He was very much a strength to Jon and myself. It would have been much more difficult if he had not been there."

The hate-America-and-Belgium campaign seemed to be stepped up. Those with Paul did not wish to mention or talk about the threats against him, but Paul doubtless knew, for on the day when Gbenye announced that the American major would be killed, Paul made a notation in his Testament, "In God's Hands." In prison, Paul had said he was the worst possible one the Simbas could have picked on, because of the article done about the Wasolo mission when Phil Littleford was with us. Therefore he knew that people in the United States knew who he was because of the publication of this article. And yet, the mob raged for "justice."

Radio Stanleyville announced that Major Carlson had been killed. Paul worried about what effects this news would have on his wife and family.

Wednesday, November 18, is a date with a hard square around it in Paul's brief diary in his Testament, with the notation, "To monument—President." The five members of the consulate staff (including the consul, Michael Hoyt), Jon Snyder, Gene Bergman, and Paul—a total of eight Americans—were taken from the prison to the Lumumba Monument amid cheering, accusing, wild mobs. This had been the scene of countless numbers of executions. Were these men to be next?

Many Congolese, officials, educated people, and enemies of the regime had had their lives taken by various means in this very spot, while the crowds watched the proceedings. As the threats against the "major" as well as all other Americans continued, the crowd went wild. What the accused eight did not know at the time was that it was to be only a mock execution, delayed apparently by rebel General Olenga; the eight were carted away again to the car and driven to President Gbenye's home. The screaming crowds followed the car.

The jeering mob demanded to know which one of the eight was the major. Paul was the only one of them who spoke an African language. "There is no major here; there are five diplomats and three missionaries," he said in Lingala. The crowd apparently thought that someone who spoke their own language certainly could not be an enemy. Each of the eight wondered, still, if the end might come now with this crowd pushing in on them, or if possibly some incident might touch things off.

They finally arrived at President Gbenye's home. Here, Gbenye referred to Paul as a major, but he did not point to him or place him before the crowd. Gbenye said at this time, however, that Paul would be killed. At this word, Paul handed his Testament to Gene, whispering, "Take this to my wife."

However, after this harassment, the eight were returned safely to the prison. Once there, Paul led them in a short prayer, thanking God for delivering them from harm that day.

On Friday they were transferred from the prison to the supposedly more comfortable quarters of the Victoria Hotel. However, with the gathering of all hostages in this one place, it was crowded. They slept in the corridors, when sleep was possible, after an afternoon and evening of harassment by crowds gathered outside, crowds yelling and screaming for the blood of the American major.

They had no sooner got settled, however, than they were herded out and into a bus and a truck. They did not know their destination—with both vehicles packed so full they were scarcely able to breathe. Was it to be their fate to be thrown into one of the large rivers that flowed near Stanleyville? Or were they to be taken to a place where they would not be found if rescue came, and then be held still longer as hostages for further negotiations? Not far out of town the bus broke down. The driver called for someone to fix it, but no one answered. Finally, a Belgian man said he would try. He fixed it—so that the bus could not move without a new part.

The hostages were herded into a small house along the road. The prisoners had heard of situations like this in which the house would be doused with gasoline and set aflame. Someone passed out; Paul thought it was a heart attack. Paul and Gene decided they had better get some rest as the night came on. The hut was so crowded and they lay down on the floor using each other's thighs for pillows.

Late in the evening a Simba official came along, saying that the hostages should not have been taken out of town. They were ordered into a passing cattle truck and went back to the hotel.

November 22 was a peaceful day. There was renewed talk of negotiations. Many in the hotel needed, if nothing else, the comfort of mind of knowing that a doctor was there, so Paul set up a small dispensary. He was able to obtain medicines as only the Americans and Belgians were being held as hostages, and many other people of other nationalities were in Stanleyville. Those who were free were permitted to take food and news to the hostages.

The missionaries met together for times of Bible study and prayer. Paul took his turn, and chose to study, from 2 Timothy, the challenge of the Apostle Paul to Timothy: "Take your share of hardship like a good soldier of Christ Jesus." Paul has underlined 2 Timothy 4:17-18: "But the Lord stood by me and lent me strength, so that I might be his instrument in making the full proclamation of the Gospel for the whole pagan world to hear, and thus I was rescued out of the lion's jaws. And the Lord will rescue me from every attempt to do me harm, and keep me safe until his heavenly reign begins."

Paul mentioned what a joy it was to be singing with a group again; he had missed fellowship and song, which always meant so much to him. Gene said they all could tell how deeply Paul felt about spiritual matters.

Paul remained cheerful. His faith was strong. He was able to be of comfort and help to those who needed him. His only entries on the 22nd and 23rd of November are: "Peace."

Relative peace pervaded in the hotel those two days. There was some comfort in that the prisoners were able to have hot baths and get cleaned up during a lull. Most important, Paul had peace within, knowing that he had committed his all to Christ, whether it meant in life or in death.

A severely beaten Belgian man was brought in from Aketi. Because an old military card had been found on his person, he had been accused of being a mercenary. Paul took care of his wounds and was allowed to leave the hotel briefly to arrange for the taking of x-rays.

As tension mounted Monday evening and the hostages knew that something would happen soon, someone asked Paul what he would do now that he had become a world figure and would probably meet President Lyndon Johnson. Paul answered very sternly, "I just take a day at a time."

The hostages in the Victoria Hotel were awakened early Tuesday morning, November 24, by the sound of airplanes. This was the day they hoped would come, and yet they dreaded it, fearing what the outcome would be. They had been threatened with death, if the planes came over. Paul was with Gene and Jon, and the three had a short prayer session, placing their lives in God's hands. Then the Simba guards came rushing in and told them all to go out in the street. There was no choice but to obey.

In a brief meeting with Chuck Davis, Paul said it might be the intention of the Simbas to use the hostages as "human shields." Chuck said later that he wondered if Paul, being on a higher floor of the hotel, had seen the paratroopers landing. Those on the lower floors had not been able to see what was going on. But that was not a time for conversation. They were made to sit down on the street while guns were firing all around the area. The Simbas grew more and more nervous.

Then rebel Colonel Opepe was shot by his own men, apparently exciting the Simbas and confusing things even more. In the mad confusion, some of the hostages were hit. Many fell, some dead and some playing dead. Others ran. They ran for the nearest protection. A small group ran to the shelter of a house and clambered over the porch wall.

Chuck Davis was by that narrow wall, where there was room for only one at a time to vault over. Paul came running alongside, saying, "Go." Chuck leaped the wall, reached back, had his fingers on Paul's sweater when a young Simba, coming around the corner with a gun, fired five shots.

Paul's work on earth was finished. His heavenly life began.

Meanwhile, in Bangui, we had the radio on. I remember Frank walking into the room, snapping it off, and going out. This incident did not alarm me, because we all knew our nerves were too taut to listen to the announcements hour after hour. It was a hot day. The children were invited across the street to the Klievers at the Brethren Mission for some lemonade. Then I saw the American ambassador, his assistant, and Frank come up the walk.

A numbness went through me as they informed me of the reports from the first plane into Leopoldville saying that Paul was now in heaven.

One by one, our missionaries came in to join me. I remember glancing up through tear-filled eyes to see one of our missionaries—a tall, large-built man—coming up the gravel walk. Just the night before he had had such assurance that Paul's life would be spared. Now he came up the walk, his long arms drooping at his side, his head hung low. We sat together and prayed. We prayed for both courage and guidance; for wisdom to tell the children; for others who were being left alone, we knew not who at this time.

My thoughts went to the Congolese at Wasolo. Paul had come out to serve, yet he had spent so little time with them. Why? I asked. Why, O why, after so many years of training, had he had so little time in which to serve? Then the thought came to me: Our time is not God's time. God does not count service in terms of years.

It was evening before I could tell the children. My words to them were something like this:

"We have been wondering where Daddy is, and waiting for him for a long time. It will be a while yet before we see him, because Jesus took him to heaven this morning."

There were tears. Then Wayne said, "Well, Mom, now at least we know where he is."

In Stanleyville that morning it was several minutes before Chuck Davis knew what actually had happened to Paul. He later said that when he saw Paul lying there, "I fell down and cried like a baby."

Gene saw Paul fall. As the rounds of shooting subsided in the immediate area but were continuing nearby, he went over to Paul. He saw Paul's Testament in his pocket, and gently removed it, for he knew Paul's wish that it be returned to me.

The Italian consul, upon hearing that Paul was dead, threw his arms around Gene Bergman and exclaimed, "Why did it have to be him?"

A Belgian co-prisoner said simply, "There was a man."

Because he had been a national figure, a symbol of the hostages, his burden at times was very heavy. Life on this earth fled in an instant. "Amen. Come, Lord Jesus!" is underlined in Paul's Testament (Revelation 22:20).

X I

Return to the Ubangi

"Though the answer is not what we would have hoped, we know that our God is too loving to be unkind and too wise to err." This was one of the many messages I received within the first few hours and days after Paul's death.

Telegrams came from President Lyndon B. Johnson, from the United States ambassador in Leopoldville, from the United States ambassador in Bangui, from the president of the Central African Republic, from friends and relatives. Messages came from many people we had never met. It was a great comfort to know that we were in the thoughts and prayers of so many persons scattered throughout the world.

Thursday, November 26, Thanksgiving Day, the Monsons, the children, and I were invited to the home of the Brays, an embassy family, for a turkey dinner. No one felt festive, but the children especially enjoyed the turkey—the first turkey in two years for them. The turkeys had been sent in for the embassy staff, and we were grateful to be included in the invitation.

Later that afternoon, Edward Brennan, from the embassy, came over to our house and said, "Lois, we have heard from the embassy in Leopoldville that Paul's body and the bodies of the others from Stanleyville have been flown to Leopoldville, and you will be able to have a choice of where you want Paul to rest." He paused for a moment. "Arrangements can be made to have him sent back to the United States, or remain in Leopoldville, or possibly, be returned to the Ubangi, if that would be your choice."

This news came as a surprise to me, because I knew what had been the fate of others in similar circumstances in the fighting in Congo. I knew plans had been made for the children and me to fly to Leopoldville to meet Paul whenever he might be released. It was very difficult knowing that we would have to meet in such a way. Still, it was a comfort in knowing where his earthly body would rest. On that Thanksgiving Day, I breathed a prayer of thanks to God for letting us know this much, for allowing us this opportunity.

Paul's family had sent a telegram saying that, above all, my wishes should come first. There was no time for a telegram to be sent back now. Instantly, I knew the place Paul would have chosen—the cemetery near the Karawa station where other missionaries who had lost their lives in the Ubangi were lying.

One of our missionary teachers whose life was snuffed out during her first term of service by a bolt of lightning rests there. An infant son of Dr. Almquist's lies there. Bob Thornbloom's young sister also lies in this spot. Another young person, named Clyde Carlson, rests there, too, along with others who went to be with the Lord in years gone by. Yes, certainly, Paul would have chosen that spot.

I told Mr. Brennan my decision; yet there was no assurance that these plans could be carried out because, in the strife, the Ubangi still was forbidden territory for Americans to enter.

"What chance do you think there is that these plans can be carried out?" asked Frank.

"I'd say better than a fifty-fifty chance," Mr. Brennan replied.

Frank turned to Byron Seashore next to him and said, "Let's be on our way. We should be in Gemena when that plane comes in tomorrow."

It was late afternoon—almost time for the last barge to cross the Ubangi River into Ubangi Province. Frank and Byron had to get across on that barge if they were to make Gemena in time. Mr. Brennan just nodded silently. He did not stop them. I did not dare ask if I would be allowed to go in.

Friday morning a call came to me from Los Angeles. It was Dwight. Dwight's voice sounds so much like Paul's over the telephone that I didn't know how I was going to be able to talk to him, but I knew I must. This was a long way to call, and I thought immediately, "What if the family is objecting to my decision?"

As I took the call, Art Lundblad, from our mission, came in, giving me the thumbs-up sign, and I knew that word had come from Leopoldville that the plane carrying Paul was leaving on the way to Gemena. The entire Carlson family—Mom and Dad Carlson, Dwight, Paul's sister Sharon—were in whole-hearted agreement with my decision, I learned with relief. It was then that I was given news of Mom Carlson's heart attack, but was assured that she was getting along all right.

Preparations had to be completed quickly, because arrangements were being made for funeral services at eleven o'clock in Karawa on Saturday, the next day. Art went to the airport, where he found a small plane with a pilot who was willing to fly eight or nine of us into Gemena. It was felt that a truck ride would be a little too difficult for me. Personally I was wondering how I could stand a bumpy, twelve-hour ride. I was feeling very weak and tired.

That day, many of our missionaries from outlying stations were arriving in Bangui for a business meeting. The timing seemed just right. All wanted to proceed on into the Ubangi for the services. The embassy said, "We cannot give you permission, but we will not stop you." That seemed to be the signal for all to be on their way. So it was that another mission truck left for the long trek into the Ubangi.

It would have been a great day of rejoicing had they been entering under other circumstances.

Early Saturday morning, the plane with Wayne, Lynette, myself, and six other missionaries left for the hour-long flight to the Gemena airport. There was no radio from ground to airplane, so we had to fly by landmarks. As we approached what was thought to be the Gemena airport, all was fogged in. The plane circled, and circled again. Now that we had come this far, were we not to land?

Suddenly there was a clearing, the plane dipped, and down we came on the runway at Gemena. The whole town of Gemena was out to meet us. I was surprised to see so many Europeans still there. I thought they had all left. There to greet us were all the *commerçants*, the father superior of the Catholic mission of our area, Congolese government and military officials, as well as countless numbers of Congolese.

We proceeded to our Gemena mission station for a brief rest before climbing into the vehicles for the nearly two-hour-long drive to Karawa. A *commerçant* came with his car for the children and me, Margaret, and Art Lundblad. This was a privileged method of travel in this area—we traveled always by truck—but it seemed that everyone wanted to make things as comfortable as possible for us.

For months there had been roadblocks in the Ubangi. Travelers had to answer questions by soldiers concerning where they were going and why; sometimes they had to show traveling papers. This day, the roadblocks went up. We said simply, "Going to Karawa." The word was out, and everyone knew where all the vehicles were headed that Saturday morning.

There seemed to be a mass movement of all Gemena vehicles toward Karawa. There was no question of charges for rides. If there was room, and someone wanted to go, he hopped on the truck and went. All wanted to pay their respects to Monganga Paul.

As we approached Palm Lane at Karawa, we saw that flowers and bright-colored leaves had been tied to the trunk of each palm tree. Children were standing along the road, holding bright flowers and colored leaves in their hands. What a beautiful sight. Margaret and I couldn't help but shed some tears.

I looked at the beautiful bouquet of red and rose carnations in my lap, which we were bringing from Bangui. How Paul loved flowers; how he loved the beauties of nature; how he loved beauty. There were flowers everywhere. They must have picked every franzy-pansy on the Karawa station. There were franzy-pansies bordering the lane leading to the church. There were bright flowers and leaves on the archways. Almost all the people along the way were holding flowers.

In front of the church were several sprays of flowers, and when we went inside, on the plain wooden casket we saw a large spray of native flowers. Alongside that spray, I placed our bouquet of red and rose carnations—the only flowers available that day in Bangui. A large white bow held these flowers together, and on it was the word "BELOVED" in gold letters.

Yes, Monganga Paul had returned to those he loved. Certainly not in the manner that all had hoped and prayed, but he had returned to them. The Congolese wish always to be buried in their own village. Because Paul had been returned to their village, they truly felt that he was one of them. I was told that at six o'clock that morning the pastors and leaders had held a prayer service around Paul's body. One of the teachers, as he prayed, asked God's forgiveness: he had always thought that missionaries came out for some sort of glory for themselves, but now he knew that they were not afraid to die for them, and he pled forgiveness for his earlier lack of comprehension.

The crowds gathered for the funeral service, and the Karawa church was filled to overflowing. People squeezed together on the low benches, to make room for more than ordinarily would fit. As the church was open on the sides, others gathered along the outside edges. This was a service completely planned and led by the Congolese pastors and leaders.

Enoc Sakofio, the hunchbacked school director of Karawa schools, opened the service with prayer and then a congregational song, "In the Sweet By and By." During the last strains of this song, we heard the shuffle of soldiers' footsteps. I had seen many soldiers around the church as we entered, and I was told that they were from the local post. I had for a moment the thought, "They've come to get us all! But little does it matter, as we'll all meet together." No sooner had these thoughts passed through my mind than I realized that they were the official contingent of soldiers from Gemena forming an honor guard at the front of the church around Paul's casket, to give him the full military honors of the Republic of Congo. The Bible school choir from Goyongo had been brought over by Jim Monson to sing "Nearer My God to Thee."

Pastor Zacharie Alengi, president of the Evangelical Church of the Ubangi, gave the funeral message. He talked about how death had come as a result of the sin that had entered the Garden of Eden, saying that death, which comes for all people, had stolen this brother from them. He recalled going to Wasolo for Flossie's wedding, and that was the last time he had seen the doctor.

He told of being greeted by Dr. Paul, who brought them in himself and helped take care of their food and helped them get bedded down. Dr. Paul had told them then that if he had to leave they would know that he wouldn't go far and that he would come back as soon as possible. "I saw this was love," said Pastor Alengi, "and I asked myself, 'Why did this doctor choose a place like this?' It came from love and joy." And then to all assembled: "On the day of resurrection, will you see the doctor?"

Pastor Alengi talked about the resurrection and of the powers of death, and how on resurrection day we should see the doctor. "Be ready for that day," he said. Then he read 1 Thessalonians 4:13-18 especially for the children and me, saying, "We do not have to grieve like those who have no hope beyond the grave, for since we believe that Jesus died and rose again, even so, God will also bring with him, through Jesus, those who have fallen asleep in death. The Lord himself will descend from heaven, and those who have departed this life in Christ will rise first. Then we, who are still living, shall be caught up to meet the Lord. And so always, through the eternity of eternities, we shall be with the Lord. Therefore comfort and encourage one another with these words."

Dan Ericson, one of our missionaries in Leopoldville, who had accompanied Paul's body, gave the eulogy in French. He related some of the things that the refugees in Stanleyville had told him about Paul. "Dr. Paul gave himself faithfully to his task," he said. "He gave of his spiritual strength to those who had fear." He told of those who credited their rescue to Dr. Paul because of the worldwide attention focused on him. His name had become a symbol of all the hostages.

Dan spoke of the New Testament that Paul had carried with him, which had been retrieved by the Mennonite missionaries and brought out of Stanleyville. "It is incomprehensible that after all the suffering, his life was taken at the moment he jumped the wall to be saved. But the Lord does not make mistakes, and we cannot question his wisdom or doubt his love. We are shocked and sad, but our sadness is transformed into joy because of our faith in Jesus Christ, who gives eternal life."

The government's minister of the interior in the Ubangi Province then read a statement about Paul's work in the Ubangi, saying how much it had meant to the people, and how sad they were that he had been called from his work with them.

Frank had asked me before the service if I would be willing—or felt I had the strength—to say a few words to the people, because it would mean so much to them for me to speak. I said, "Frank, I just don't know."

Prior to the service, I had met Pastor Bangi from Wasolo. We could not speak, but put our arms around each other, and buried our heads on each other's shoulders and wept. How could I possibly say anything to the crowd gathered?

Somehow I felt a strength beyond my own, and I felt I must say something to the people, so I got to my feet, went forward, and turned to face them: "My husband came here because he loved you. He saw the great medical need and wanted to serve, both medically and spiritually. Why his time among you was so short we do not know, but God knows. Each of us has a time to be called home. God has called my husband, Paul. I leave his physical body here as a reminder and memorial to you people whom he loved so dearly. I know he would have chosen to stay with you. May we always carry on the medical and spiritual work for our dear, loving heavenly Father here in Congo.

"Though my children and I must return to America, a part of my heart will always remain here. May God bless you." Frank then took Paul's New Testament and read several of the verses that had been underlined, and said that on November 23 Paul's entry was: "Peace." Then Frank said, "And Lois, for you and the children, I would like to add this: 'Tuesday, November 24: Perfect Peace.'"

Pastor Bangi offered prayer. The honor guard presented arms, played "Taps," and marched out. The band from Goyongo played, "My Jesus I Love Thee." The pastors had chosen to be pallbearers, but the soldiers felt it was their right and their privilege to be pallbearers, also, so the pastors and the soldiers shared in this responsibility.

The funeral procession to the small cemetery a few kilometers from the church was a long one, with a variety of cars and trucks such as I had never seen in my days in Congo. Scores of people were on foot besides. It was a large crowd, but all was orderly and quiet. The honor guard stood at attention. There was the brief final ceremony and prayer. The soldiers presented arms, and then "Taps" was played again. Palm branches were placed on the casket, and Monganga Paul was laid to rest.

On the grave marker, in Lingala, is the verse:

> *There is no greater love than this, that a man should lay down his life for his friends.*
>
> *John 15:13*

EPILOGUE

Plans were being made for the children and me to return to the United States a few days after Paul's funeral, when Frank came to me after a mission board meeting and said, "Lois, you know you don't have to leave now if you don't want to." Immediately a heavy load was lifted! I did not want to leave. Veteran missionaries had told us before we went overseas that "Congo gets in your blood." I had hardly believed I would develop such a deep feeling—but now I knew. We were new missionaries and had not been privileged to be in the field long, but the love for Congo and the Congolese was deep in my blood.

A high hill rises outside the city of Bangui. Frequently we drove to the top where, from one vantage point, we could look across the Ubangi River to the hills of Congo. Beyond those hills live thousands in a land of turmoil, thousands who cry for help, for guidance, for education, for the healing of broken bodies and bleeding hearts—crying for those who will come to help with love—not those who come only to deceive and exploit. I thought as I gazed across, beyond the hills, farther than my eyes could see, to the cemetery where Paul's earthly body will remain in the village of the Congolese until resurrection morning, of how he had once referred to Congo as the "promised land." Yes, a beautiful land, a rich land—a land of promise!

As I accompanied the children north about 200 miles into the Central African Republic so they could finish the semester of school, I learned how closely the Africans of this country also had followed the news of Congo and about my husband. Though they had never seen him they knew that he had come to serve their brothers and sisters and they were in deep sorrow. Again, they spoke a different language, but as they came to the missionary home where I stayed there was always someone near at hand who could translate for us. They all voiced much the same thoughts as the message given to me by Enoc Sakofio, the Congolese director of the Karawa schools. In part he said:

> We have indeed sustained a great loss. Paul is lost to us as if from our hands. Paul came to do two things, he came to teach us the good news of God, and he came to heal our diseases.... Paul had both of these tasks to do, but he has died in our hands and it gives us much sorrow. Whoever shot Paul didn't kill "him"; he killed "us." Look today at Wasolo, at those people carried in on the litters so that Paul might heal them. But now who will heal them? They are dying there. It isn't white people who are dying there but we black people who are dying. That person didn't kill Paul; he killed us....
>
> Paul died an honorable death. Paul died for his people. As Jesus said in John 10:11, "I will die for my sheep." So Paul died for us. He died alone, but today scores of those who might have been healed by Paul have died. And so it goes day by day. But Paul died in a day.
>
> Send a letter to his mother and father and his relatives and say that we are glad they agreed that he be buried among us. When we go by we will see his grave because he agreed to die among us. He didn't want to leave us and for that those who killed him did not kill him, but us.
>
> We prayed and prayed for Paul, with sorrow, with weariness. People sat by their radios and listened to hear if Paul had been released, or what should happen to Paul. We prayed much. But God's will was done, not the will of man. Let us thank God for what he has done.

Because Paul had been called for permanent service in Congo by the Evangelical Church of the Ubangi, they feel a deep responsibility for his death. President Zacharie Alengi expressed their feeling in these words: "Truly we have great sorrow because of the death of our brother, because we know his humility, kindness, and desire to help us Congolese, both in our bodies and in our souls. Although his desire was only to help us, the people of Congo, yet he was killed here. Therefore we give testimony to the fact that unless we give ourselves completely to God his blood will be upon us. The death of the doctor brought much praise and glory to God here in the Congo and in the whole world. For us and our children it will be a symbol which does not end."

The governor of the Ubangi Province, who had not been able to attend the funeral, sent me a letter, which reads in part: "My Minister of the Interior has told you in behalf of the government how the people of the Ubangi sorrow because of the terrible and unmerited death of him who had given himself devotedly for them in caring for their physical needs as a doctor. For my part, I am not able to add anything to this, for I know that no human word will ever be able to comfort you in the loss of a husband, one who was removed from the love of his own by tragic and inhuman circumstances.

"However, if this is able to be of comfort to you, I am able to assure you that the sacrifice of your husband will not have been in vain. In fact, the grave where he rests in a village of our Province will remain always as a reminder to us that in the midst of the hatred and violence that troubled our Congo, a man willingly gave himself to die (to make the supreme sacrifice) for an ideal of peace, love and brotherhood among men."

In January, it became imperative that we should return to the United States. As I was packing, Lynette said, "Mommy, I really wish we were going back to Wasolo." How thankful I was to know that our children were left with fond memories of our life together at our mission station. I knew in my heart that Paul would have been thankful for this also. My thoughts turned to other children whose minds have been left scarred by horrors which they have seen. How my heart ached as I prayed that the Lord would remove the scars and memories.

We returned by way of Brussels so we could visit Florence and Paul Sedua who had become established in a small apartment and were going to school. They were so happy to see us. Paul Sedua had written a letter previous to this, regarding what we had done for them in connection with their wedding: "I do not know how I can thank you for all you did for Florence, for you gave yourselves completely for her and you treated her as if she were your own daughter. In our whole lives, we will never forget what you did for us. And what you did for her, it is as though you did it for me, for she is now my wife and so I thank you many times over. . . . Your kindness touches us very much. That is why, if Florence begins to think about you, she just cries and cries. It is very sad—but we will meet again."

Several of the Belgian priests who were with Paul sent their expressions of condolence. Father Prosper De Swaef—who was injured severely at Wapinda, and whom Paul persuaded the rebels not to take—wrote, "I will never forget this good doctor who is so sadly the victim of his own devotion, and . . . I think often of your great sorrow and the sorrow of your children. I pray that the good Lord will help you in your sorrow."

Father Leon Delaere, bishop of Molegbe in the Ubangi, wrote, "During the hours of anguish which preceded the fatal moment of his death, we all prayed for his liberation, and even more so since he was a prisoner together with three of our priests from whom we have heard nothing.

"We are moved as we think of the death of that other brave man, so tragically killed, who was the president of the United States: Kennedy. Dead hardly one year ago . . . his memory remains as a benediction to our hearts."

In June 1965 I heard again from Father Delaere and I was saddened to be informed of the cruel deaths of the three priests from Yakoma who had been taken with Paul—Pères Leopold Neyens, Monulphe Schrijvers, and Adrien Van Den Broucke. They were killed in Buta in the terrible massacre of May 30, after nine months of captivity.

From England, Rev. Geoffrey Farrand, pastor of the Highfield Congregational Church in Rock Ferry, wrote: "As a church we honor the memory of Dr. Paul Carlson, who went out to the Congo two years ago. The news of his death came as a sad blow to us all. We only knew him personally for the three months he was studying in Merseyside, though during that time he was never absent from worship. We heard him speak to the church and to the Senior Department of Family Church. Some of us had him in our homes. He was a most likable man, with all the vitality and informality we think of as being typically American, but coupled with a sincerity, a humility, and a burning love of Christ which left a deep impression on us."

And again from Congo, from Gebanga Joseph, Wasolo schoolteacher who took over the responsibilities as director of the Wasolo schools: "At that time we saw that the death of Dr. Paul was like the death of Jesus, for when Gbenye asked the rebels what he should do with Paul Carlson, they all cried out: 'Kill this American—Imperialist!' We know that he should have escaped, but it was not the will of God, for there were many together with him in jail in Stanleyville, and because of Dr. Paul, many of them were saved. The death of Paul gives to the church at Wasolo the power of the Holy Spirit that we might preach the Good News. Because of this we have reopened the hospital and the schools.

"I desire to come to America to tell of the influence of Dr. Paul but the road is long and where would I get the money? Greet the church in America from the church here at Wasolo. Even though Dr. Paul has been taken away, we are not growing weary of the message of God."

Wonderful letters came from literally all over the world to Paul's family and to me and the children. How grateful we are to those who wrote and to the thousands who upheld all of us in prayer. I know that Paul and the other prisoners as well as ourselves felt strongly the power of prayer. I am constantly reminded of how far-reaching was this news story of November 1964, of how many thousands all over the world have now heard of Wasolo, the "forgotten corner," of how many thousands have been reminded of the work of missionaries throughout the world, of how many thousands have read Paul's words in print and heard his voice on tape. He could never have dreamed of telling the story of Christ and the cause of missions to so many—then, through his death, he has spoken and continues to speak to countless numbers.

In this age when so many still doubt the existence of Christ and a God who rules the universe, there also are untold numbers of us who believe that God is the Supreme Ruler and he uses men and women who are committed to him to speak to those who do not believe.

Some would say that it was by chance that Dr. Warren Berggren became ill and had to go home, thereby bringing Philip Littleford, medical student on a Smith, Kline & French fellowship, to Wasolo under the sponsorship of Dr. Paul Carlson; that by chance a photographer was sent out to shoot approximately 1,000 pictures for an article to appear in a large American newspaper about the work in the "forgotten corner" of the Ubangi—where no one ever comes—so that many knew, before the rebel propaganda of Radio Stanleyville began, that Dr. Paul Carlson existed; that by chance he was used as a symbol of all the hostages in Congo; that by chance, just a moment before he would have reached safety, he was felled by bullets from the gun of a young rebel who had no idea who he was.

No, not by chance. God could have got him safely over the wall in Stanleyville just as so many times before he had kept Paul safe from the "jaws of the lion." I am convinced that God chose to take Paul at that moment to be with him.

Our days may be short or long—this fact is brought vividly before me with Paul's death and each day as I read the paper. So many people have asked me, "But why were Paul's days cut so short when doctors are so desperately needed?" God knows how much Paul was needed as a doctor, but he found he had need of Paul at that particular time and place for his purposes. I have peace in this assurance.

AFTERWORD

Within seven months of Paul Carlson's death, Covenant missionaries began returning to Congo. Among those who returned were doctors like Helen Berquist and Theodora "Teddy" Johnson, who, as Paul did, felt an overwhelming sense that God had called them to serve the people of Congo. They had preceded Paul to the Congo, and, along with the missionary doctors and nurses that followed them, would continue with the ministry despite great difficulties.

Lois Carlson returned to Congo in 1966 on a medical survey mission. She and Paul's brother, Dwight, were traveling on behalf of the Paul Carlson Medical Program (PCMP), a foundation started in his memory. Their destination was an abandoned hospital near the village of Loko, ninety kilometers east of Karawa. Built by the Belgians just prior to independence, the hospital had never been opened.

Paul and Lois had visited the hospital soon after arriving in Congo in 1963. With 140 beds, it dwarfed the small hospital at Wasolo, and Paul began to dream of making it a Covenant medical center. But the project seemed far beyond the Covenant's reach. Still, Paul wrote to L. Arden Almquist, then head of Covenant World Mission, about the Loko hospital and its possibilities.

The idea stuck with Almquist, a former missionary doctor who had worked in Wasolo for nearly a decade. After Paul's death, Almquist, with Lois's help, organized the Carlson foundation and felt the hospital near Loko was the perfect place to start.

During her visit to Congo, Lois met with then President Mobutu, who agreed to deed the hospital to the foundation. The hospital was repaired under the supervision of Dr. Wallace and Sarah Thornbloom, the project's first directors, and other Covenant missionaries. In March 20, 1968, the 140-bed Institut Medical Evangelique Doctor Carlson (IMEDOCA) was dedicated to the memory of Paul Carlson. (Dr. Titus Johnson ran the hospital after Wallace Thornbloom's heart attack in 1969.) In 1973, Almquist moved to Loko and assumed the role of medical director. The hospital would later become known as the Institut Medical Evangelique de Loko (IMELOKO).

More than just a hospital, IMELOKO was a holistic approach to community health. Eventually fifteen satellite clinics were set up in villages, staffed by Congolese nurses and equipped with solar-powered refrigerators to store medicines. Agricultural projects were started on the 200 acres that surrounded the hospital, growing beans, coffee, oil palm, cocoa, and fruit trees, with seeds made available to local farmers. Cattle bred to resist tropical disease were raised, and more than 6,000 village fishponds were started to raise tilapia fish.

Through IMELOKO, as Arden Almquist put it in a history of the PCMP, God had transformed "the tragedy of Dr. Paul's death into blessings for thousands of people in Central Africa. Surely that is the dream come true."

By the mid-1990s the Covenant Church of Congo (CEUM), with more than 100,000 members was thriving. The health system, with four hospitals (Karawa, Bokado, Wasolo, and IMELOKO), and more than seventy clinics in villages, was one of the finest in the country. Many of the doctors and nurses were Congolese, trained by the Covenant medical school at Karawa. More than 27,000 children attended CEUM-run schools. The projects developed at IMELOKO had led to a level of sustainable economic development-farmers had crops in the field and the means to transport their harvest to market.

All of this had been accomplished despite growing unrest caused by the overwhelming corruption under President Mobutu. During more than thirty years in office, Mobutu stole billions from the national treasury while the country's infrastructure slowly disintegrated. His power began to crumble in 1991, following riots in Kinshasa by disenchanted soldiers that sparked ongoing unrest. That same year, the entire Covenant missionary staff—eighty-five adults and children—were forced to evacuate Congo (then known as Zaire). They would return in 1992 and continue the process of intentionally turning leadership of the ministry over to CEUM leaders, until being forced to evacuate again in late 1996 and early 1997.

From 1996 to 2002, a civil war raged in Congo, with rebels backed by soldiers and funding from Zimbabwe, Libya, Chad, Angola, Namibia, Uganda, and Rwanda fighting for control of Congo. When Mobutu was driven from power in 1997, the country collapsed into chaos. According to the International Rescue Committee, more than 2.5 million people in Congo died during the conflict from violence, starvation, and disease. It became known as "Africa's First World War." During the war, rebels and foreign mercenaries ransacked hospitals, burned schools and homes to the ground, and stole nearly everything of value.

The CEUM, now 178,000 strong, has refused to give up hope in the midst of almost unthinkable privation. The church's schools, despite lacking even the most basic supplies such as pencils and paper, remained open and now serve more than 49,000 students. The teachers, who were not paid their government salaries for years, refused to give up. The four hospitals also remained open, the medical staff often working without pay, with damaged equipment and medicines in short supply, and fighting epidemics of AIDS, malaria, sleeping sickness, and other diseases as a result of the war. The Covenant medical system, with its eleven Congolese doctors and 173 nurses, serves an estimated one million people.

Following a 2002 peace agreement, a sense of stability has returned to Congo, and the CEUM has begun the long rebuilding process. The foundation started in Paul's memory has been reborn as the Paul Carlson Partnership (PCP) to assist in this effort. It is a true partnership, bringing Covenanters from northwest Congo and North America together to help bring Paul Carlson's dream back to life.

Focused on health, poverty eradication, and education, the PCP has launched a three-year, five million dollar fundraising effort to rebuild hospitals and schools in northwest Congo, part of the ongoing witness to the love of God in Jesus Christ that marked Pau's life. (More details about the partnership can be found be found at www.covchurch.org.)

It was the love of God that brought Paul to Congo, and the desire to witness to that love that sustained his work at Wasolo and gave him hope till the end.

Speaking at a 1964 memorial service for Paul in Chicago, Arden Almquist summarized Paul's life this way: "Paul Carlson was a dedicated believer in Jesus Christ as Savior and Lord. As Savior, because he know that apart from the indwelling in Christ in his life, he himself was capable, as every man is, of doing the kind of ugly things that men did to him in his own final weeks of suffering and death. He accepted the fact that he himself was a sinner, and that this is why Jesus died, and joyously embraced the wondrous grace of God."

What made Paul different was that "he was not content to regard Christ as Savior alone. He obeyed him as Lord," Almquist said. "Most of us are content with a formula of faith that declares we believe in Christ as Savior. We fail to acknowledge him as Lord, and so we fail to obey. Paul Carlson took Christ as his example. And what does that earlier Paul, the first Christian missionary to the Gentile world, say of Christ? He says that 'he did not cling to his prerogatives as God's equal, but stripped himself of all privilege by consenting to be a slave.'

"Paul Carlson did not cling to his prerogatives as a western man, educated in anthropology, trained as a physician and surgeon, certified in tropical medicine and the French language. He stripped himself of the privileges which his cultural and educational background qualified him to exercise, and became a servant of the Congolese people."

Paul's legacy extends far beyond Congo, as he inspired many who heard his story to follow his example of service. As recounted in the beginning of *Monganga Paul*, Paul once dropped everything and drove through the night to go to the aid of his friends Warren and Gretchen Berggren. The Berggrens, both Free Church missionary doctors, were in Tandala, some 330 miles from Wasolo. Warren lay near death from malaria and pneumonia, and Gretchen was out of treatment options. Bringing a dose of intravenous quinine with him, Paul saved Warren's life.

The Berggrens never forgot Paul's act of kindness. They returned to the U.S., and after studying at Harvard School of Public Health, spent more than thirty years at a hospital in rural Haiti. Because of public health improvements they started, the lives of thousands of Haitian children were saved. They also taught at Harvard and worked on public health projects around the world, which brought them in contact with "many wonderful people," says Gretchen Berggren, including meeting Mother Teresa twice. "But that," she says, "was secondary to knowing Paul Carlson."

Where are they now?

After returning home from Congo, Lois Carlson Bridges spent a number of years traveling and speaking about her experiences in Congo. She met Hank Bridges at Rolling Hills Covenant Church in California, and they were married in 1967. They were married for twenty-four years until Hank's death in 1991. She is a member of Clairemont Covenant Church in San Diego.

Wayne Carlson is a doctor in family practice. Married to Becky (Fondell) Carlson, whose parents were Covenant missionaries in Alaska, he lives outside of Chicago.

Lyn Carlson graduated from Stanford University, where she studied journalism and subsequently worked in that field and in social services. She is active in outreach ministry at her church and resides in San Diego.

Dwight Carlson is a retired psychiatrist and published author in Southern California.

Jody LeVahn, Paul's colleague at Wasolo, retired in 1996 after forty years in Congo. She received the first Paul Carlson Award from the Evangelical Covenant Church in July 2004. She lives in Minneapolis.

Christophe Gbenye, leader of the Simbas, escaped to the Central African Republic at the end of the rebellion. He became a successful businessman and was eventually allowed to return to Congo. He lives today in Kinshasa.

GLOSSARY

Bangui (bahng-gee) The capital of the Central African Republic, where Lois Carlson and the children waited for word of Paul. The rest of the missionaries had evacuated to this city.

Banzyville (bahn-zee-ville) Town along the Ubangi River on the way to Gbado. At best, a six-hour ride from Wasolo.

Bau (bow, as in "wow") One of the mission stations at the west end of the field.

Bili (bee-lee) One of the two rivers northeast of Wasolo that the rebels crossed.

Bokada (boh-kah-dah) Mission station due west of Wasolo where Teddy Johnson and Harvey and Ruth Widman worked.

Bondo (bon-doh) A town along the Uele River where Paul was taken shortly after his capture.

Bosobolo (boh-soh-boh-loh) Government hospital where Paul spent a month in 1961 relieving Warren and Gretchen Berggren.

Bumba (boom-bah) Town on the Congo River due south of Wasolo where Carl and Vivian Edstrom worked.

Businga (boo-sing-gah) Town on the Mongala River midway between Gbado and Karawa stations. The Carlsons made purchases here almost every trip to Karawa.

Buta (boo-tah) Fairly large town with a large Catholic mission to which Paul was taken and where he was free for one month.

capitani (kap-ih-tan-ee) Large whitefish sometimes weighing over thirty pounds. They were caught in the Ubangi River.

Dongbe (dong-bee) Village across the Uele River, accessible only by canoe. The Carlsons crossed the river to visit the church there and give inoculations.

Gbado (bah-doh) Mission station nearest to Wasolo where Frank and Margaret Lindquist worked and where the Carlsons always stopped on their way to Karawa.

Gemena (geh-men-ah) Capital of the Ubangi Province. Several missionaries were stationed there.

Goyongo (goh-young-oh) Mission station where the Bible school and seminary were located.

Kala (kah-lah) Station farthest from Wasolo at opposite end of the Ubangi region. Naomi Skoglund and several other missionaries were stationed there for teaching in the secondary school for the Congolese.

Karawa (kair-ah-wah) The largest mission station, with a hospital for nurses' training, a large primary school and girls' school for the Congolese, and the Ubangi Academy for the missionary children.

Kemba (kem-bah) Village in the Central African Republic directly across the river from Yakoma to which Lois, Jody LeVahn, and the children evacuated.

Kwada (kwah-dah) A spring-fed lake where the missionaries vacationed.

La Jeunesse (lah june-ess) French for "young people," a Communist-inspired movement in Congo.

Leopoldville The capital of Congo, and the country's largest city, it was renamed Kinshasa in 1966.

Libenge (li-beng-gee) A government post and hospital close to the Kala station.

Lingala (ling-gah-lah) The trade language used in our area and the official language of the Congolese National Army.

Lisala (li-sah-lah) An important port along the Congo River bordering the Ubangi region.

mai na Mulele (my-na-moo-lay-lee) "Water of Mulele," supposedly a magic potion anointing the bodies of the Simbas so that bullets could not penetrate them.

Mbomu (boh-moo) A river forming part of the boundary of the Central African Republic. One of the three rivers forming the Ubangi River.

mbote (mm-boh-teh) Word for "hello," "greetings" in Lingala.

Molegbe (moh-leg-bee) Town with a large Catholic mission between Banzyville and Gbado.

Monga (mong-gah) Village across the Uele and Bili rivers through which Paul was taken.

monganga (mong-gahng-gah) Word for "doctor" or "medicine man" in Lingala.

Mongbandi (mong-bahn-dee) A person from the Ngbandi tribe in the Wasolo area.

Ndako na kelekpa (dah-koh nah ke-lek-pah) House of the locally made low bamboo beds.

Ngbaka (nn-bah-kah) Largest tribe in the Ubangi around the Karawa, Gemena areas.

Ngunde (goon-de) Village where the road from Wasolo and the road from Yakoma meet.

Nzale (zah-leh) Large fishing village along the Ubangi River where there was a dispensary supplied by the Wasolo hospital.

pirogue (pee-rohg) A wooden dugout canoe made from an entire tree trunk.

Simba (sim-bah) Swahili for "lion." The rebels or supporters of Mulele called themselves "Simbas."

Stanleyville A port city on the Congo River in north central Congo. It was renamed Kisangani in 1966.

Tandala (tahn-dah-lah) Mission station south of Gemena with a 120-bed hospital where Warren and Gretchen Berggren worked.

Targini (tahr-gee-nee) Village about five miles from Wasolo where the small road from Wasolo connected to the main road between the towns of Bumba and Yakoma.

Ubangi (yoo-bahng-gee) The river forming the boundary between part of the Republic of Congo and the Central African Republic. Also the mission region in which the Covenant and Free Church worked.

Uele (yoo-ay-lee) River nearest to Wasolo. One of the three forming the Ubangi River.

Wapinda (wah-pin-dah) Village with a Catholic mission and dispensary about forty miles from Wasolo.

Wasolo (wah-soh-loh) Mission station where the Carlsons and Jody LeVahn worked. Extreme northeast corner of the Ubangi Province.

Yakoma (yah-koh-mah) Town nearest to Wasolo where there were some stores.

The juncture where the Uele, Bili, and Mbomu rivers meet to form the Ubangi River.

Zongo (zon-goh) Point of entry into the Republic of Congo directly across the river from Bangui, the Central African Republic.

CENTRAL AFRICAN

Ubangi River

(Monson, Lundquist)

BANGUI

ZONGO

(Dr. "Teddy" Johnson, Widman)

BOSOBOLO

GOYONGO (38)

BOKADA (37)

MOLEGBE

BANZYVILLE

(31)

GBADO
(Lindquist, Noren)

(No transmitter)
LIBENGE

(Dr. Helen Berquist, Thornbloom, Elsie Carlson, Enos)

BUSINGA

(No transmitter)

KALA (36)
(Skoglund)

GEMENA
(33)

KARAWA
(32)

BAU
(35)

(Lundblad, Seashore)

UBANGI

(EQUATOR)

PROVINCE

TANDALA
(34)

(Berggren)

Mongala River

LISAL

Congo River

REPUBLIC OF

To Leopoldville

● M.E.U. STATIONS

------ ROADS

COQUILHATVILLE

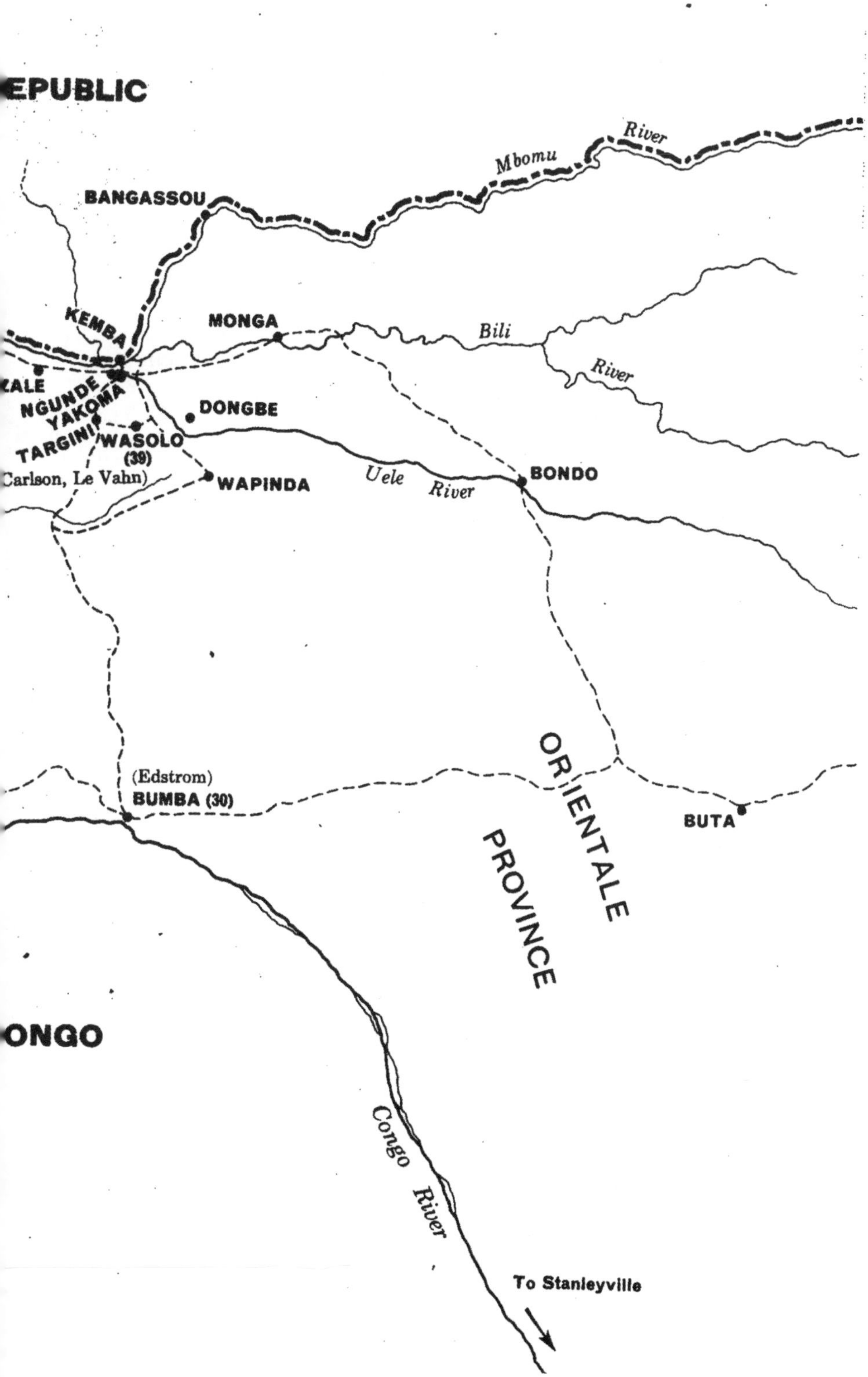

EPUBLIC

Mbomu River

BANGASSOU

KEMBA

MONGA

Bili River

ZALE
NGUNDE
YAKOMA
TARGINI
WASOLO
(39)
(Carlson, Le Vahn)

DONGBE

WAPINDA

Uele River

BONDO

ORIENTALE PROVINCE

(Edstrom)
BUMBA (30)

BUTA

ONGO

Congo River

To Stanleyville

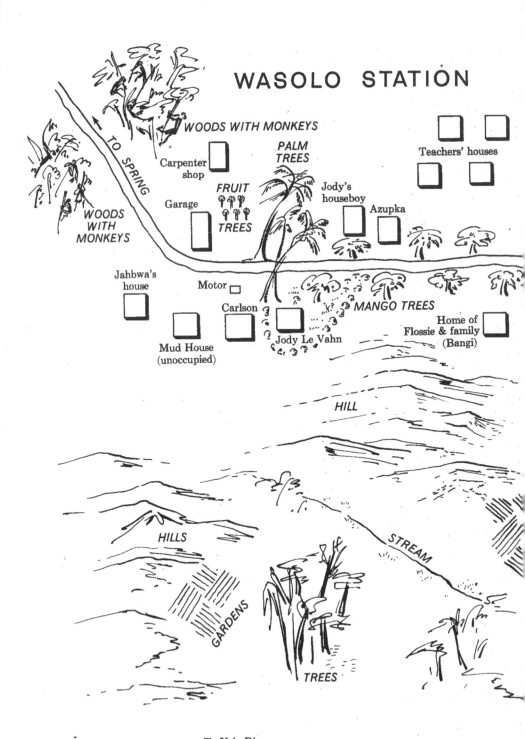

WASOLO STATION

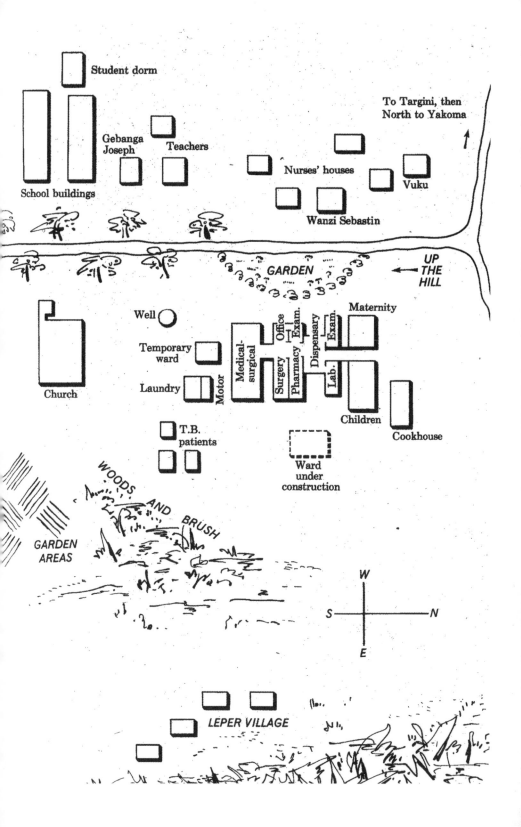